Ruy Diaz De Mendoza

I0420124

Levi Villarreal

Ruy Diaz de Mendoza

ISBN:1522735542
ISBN-13: 978-1522735540

DEDICATION

For Ruy Diaz de Mendoza

CONTENTS

Introduction

These are my notes on the genealogical investigation of Ruy Diaz de Mendoza. This is not a presentation in a traditional sense but a demonstration of my genealogical methods from beginning to end. I **only** extracted what was essential to solving this case and provided an analysis for it. The translations are mine and serve **my** purpose. I was hesitant to include chapter 11 because of the amount of information that is already available. I then decided to include it in my notes so the reader will have a guide for his/her own research. This is one the those cases where attention details and knowledge of the cultural institutions of the time matter.

1 Mendoza

Early Notes:

Mendoza- a noble family from Mendoza, Alava, Spain. They were a branch that originated with Don Inigo Lopez, Señor de Biscay. Lope Sanchez was the first Señor of llodio y Alva. His grandson Lope Iniguez is the first to use the surname Mendoza. The Mendozas rose to power during the reign Alfonso XI of Castile and the subsequent Trastamara era. Some notable Mendozas:

1. Pedro Gonzalez de Mendoza, poet and military hero. He married Aldonza de Ayala
2. Inigo Lopez de Mendoza, poet.
3. Iñigo Lopez de Mendoza, Conde de Tendilla I
4. Ynigo Lopez de Mendoza was "Conde de Tendilla II, Señor de la Valhermosa, primero Captain General de Reino de Granada", per his testimony written in 1515. He mentions his son Antonio Mendoza, who will become the first Viceroy of New Spain, and his other children are mentioned: Bernardino, Francisco, Diego, Luis, Isabel, and Pedro, the bastard son. Doña Maria and Maria Pacheco are mentioned near the end of the testament. Maria Pacheco will become famous as the leader of comunero in Toledo.

Ruy Diaz de Mendoza was a "caballero muy principal" from Baeza, Spain. His historical importance is primarily due to his relationships with important people of the 16th century. He was a duedo/pariente of the Marques de Mondejar and was married to Doña Catalina de Salazar, the daughter of Factor of New Spain Gonzalo Salazar. His granddaughter Doña Madalena de Mendoza financed the conquest of New Mexico. His grandsons Vicente Zaldivar and Juan Zaldivar were granted important military positions by their uncle Adelantado Juan de Oñate.

Who is Ruy Diaz de Mendoza? My research began in Baeza. Two books worth reading that are based on noticias, sepulchers, and memorias etc.: *Noticias y Documentos Para la Historia de Baeza* and *Nobleza de Andalucia*. After reading these books it was too far back in time to make any strong connection to Ruy Diaz de Mendoza. A quick look at the conquistadors of Baeza in 1227 reveals some information. Conquerors of Baeza:

Don Pedro Lopez

Don Diego Lopez de Haro

Pedro Sanchez Evia

Sancho Martinez

Gonzalo Diaz de Mendoza

Ruy Diaz de Mendoza

Gonzalo Diaz de Mendoza and Ruy Diaz de Mendoza are part of a list of 300 conquistadors.

Is there previous research on Ruy Diaz de Mendoza? Yes, three essays by Jose Antonio de Esquibel's *Lines of Descent from Alfonso XI, Rey de Castilla y Leon, to Ruy Diaz de Mendoza y Arellano, The Zaldivar, Diaz de Mendoza Family, and Díaz de Mendoza Mejia and Conde de Tendilla/Marqueses de Mondejar,* written for a newsletter by SHHARR in 1994 and the Los Bexarenos Genealogical Register in the year 2005.

However, his conclusion was there was not enough information to uncover the ancestry of Ruy Diaz de Mendoza. Reviewing the evidence Esquibel cited may be worthwhile.

Next Step: Reviewing the evidence of Francisco Rivadeneira and Vicente Zaldivar.

2 EVIDENCE

I will begin with the applications of Francisco Rivadeneira and Vicente Zaldivar for the Order of Santiago. The investigations covered a variety of question on candidate's ancestry. The basic questions included the origin of the candidate and parents, grandparents etc. Although, not all questions were answered by the witnesses and sometimes not in order. In general, the question included the following:

1. Their name and age. Whether or not the witness knew the candidate's parents and their names, where they were from and vecinos currently.

2. Whether or not the witness is a relative of the candidate and in what grade. If they are are friends, enemies, cuñados etc.

3. Whether or not the candidate, parents, and grandparents legitimate, legitimate marriages and births or naturals of single parents. If they are bastards in what manner does the witness know this.

4. What are the names of the parents of the candidate and father's name of the father. Whether they are hijosdalgos or not according the the customs of Spain. Whether or not they are free of bad blood (jews, conversos, moors).

5. Who are the maternal and paternal grandparents of the candidate and if they were old christians free of stain.

6.   If the candidate or his parents were a merchant or money changer.
7.   Whether or not the candidate knows how to use a horse and how does the witness know this.
8.   Has the candidate been challenged (I couldn't understand what the question was and never seen it answered).
9.   If the candidate had a bad reputation and the witness' opinion on the candidate's nobility.
10. Whether or not the candidate's direct line and maternal line were born before or after legitimate marriage. Whether or not they were condemned by the inquisition.

Evidence of Francisco Rivadeneira de Oñate
Parents:
Hernando de Rivadeneira, vecino of Valladolid and natural of Rioseco
Doña Ana Velasquez de Salazar, born in Mexico and natural of Oñate in Vizcaya
Maternal Grandparents:
Cristobal de Oñate Narria, natural of Oñate in Vizcaya
Doña Catalina Salazar, natural of Granada

August 3, 1609. In the city of Granada, on the nationality of the maternal grandmother Doña Catalina de Salazar. Don Alonso Venegas, Caballero del Habito y Orden de Santiago, vecino y Alcaide del Generalife. He gives oath.

1.   "He has hearsay information on Doña Catalina Salazar for having been a vecina and natural of this city and for having many dealings and conversations with a brother of hers named Juan Velasquez de Salazar, who was procurador general of Mexico City, New Spain; and with Ruy Diaz de Mendoza, son of Doña Catalina and Ruy Diaz de

Mendoza, her first husband. He (Ruy) was married to her in this city. She went with him to the Indias where she was widowed."

2. "Doña Catalina de Salazar, his sister (Juan Velasquez de Salazar) and for the many "noticias" that she has, she is old christian and noble and as well her distant relationship and lineage; and particularly Ruy Diaz de Mendoza, son of Doña Catalina's from her first marriage. He was married to Doña Maria Velasco. He knows and knew many caballeros named Mendoza, distant relatives of Catalina's as having been muy hijosdalgos y limpios."

On the same day and year, Captain Geronimo Davila Zaballos, vecino and natural of the city of Granada, he swears to tell the truth.

1. "He knows having met and dealt with Doña Catalina de Salazar, a natural who was of this city and was married to Ruy Diaz de Mendoza, a caballero from Baeza. The witness knew them from the casa del Marques de Mondejar in Alhambra, who was named Iñigo Lopez de Mendoza. Doña Catalina went to the Indias in the company of her husband and left her son behind in this city, who has the same name as his father. Catalina Salazar was a noblewoman and principal and her relatives were principales-- and for the treatment and courtesy that the Marques de Mondejar *gave them*. He treated them like a duedo (relative)."

One the fifteenth day of the same month and year in the same city, Gaspar Maldonado Salazar, vecino and natural of this city, gives oath.

1. "Doña Catalina was married two times. First, in Alhambra, in this city, with Ruy Diaz de Mendoza during the time of the Marques de Mondejar Don Luis, presidente of the Consejo Real."

On the seventeenth day of August of the same year, Juan Vasquez de Toledo, vecino and natural of this city, receives oath.

1. "Doña Catalina de Salazar married Ruy Diaz de Mendoza her first husband and a duedo (distant relation) to the Marques de Mondejar. She and her husband went with Don Antonio de Mendoza, Viceroy, where she was widowed"

On the same day and year of said city, Doña Michaela Tiatessia, religiosa professa in the monastery of Santiago de la Madre de Dios, receives oath to tell the truth.

1. "Catalina was married to Ruy Diaz de Mendoza, caballero muy principal…(unintelligible sentence). She went with him to the Indias, where the witness heard she (Catalina) became a widow."

On the eighteenth day of the same and year in the same city Doña Leonor Mendoza, monja professa del monastery of Santiago de la Madre de Dios in the city of Granada, gives oath to tell the truth.

1. "Doña Catalina was married to a caballero from Baeza named Ruy Diaz de Mendoza and they had a child with the same name. In the Indias she was widowed."

On the same day and year. Lopez Zeron, Caballero de la Orden de Santiago, receives oath:

1. "He did not know the paternal and maternal

grandparents, and did not know where they were vecinos or naturals. He has more knowledge of Doña Catalina de Salazar the maternal grandmother of the candidate. He always heard that she was a natural of this city and was married in the city of Baeza to Ruy Diaz de Mendoza Mexia, where the witness is from."

Analysis:

1. Ruy Diaz de Mendoza was from Baeza.
2. He was related to the Marques de Mondejar.
3. Mexia is added to Ruy's surname. This is an interesting fact because the witness stated he did not know Ruy Diaz de Mendoza. This information must be kept in in context because the investigation is not about Ruy Diaz de Mendoza. The candidate is not a descendant of Ruy Diaz Mendoza.

Evidence of Maese de Campo Vicente de Zaldivar

Parents:

Vicente de Zaldivar, natural of Vitoria and resident of the City of Zacatecas.

&

Doña Magdalena de Mendoza, his legitimate wife, natural of Granada.

Maternal Grandparents:

Ruy Diaz de Mendoza & Doña Catalina Salazar, naturales of the City Granada.

In the city of Granada, October 7, 1625. Don Luis Barrio Empieza: In the city of Granada, where Doña Madalena de Mendoza, mother of the candidate; and Ruy Diaz Mendoza and Doña Catalina de Salazar, maternal grandparents, are naturals, examined 20 witnesses.

1. "They all knew Ruy Diaz de Mendoza, veinticuatro of the said city, and Tesorero (treasurer) who went to the casa de Moneda de Mexico. They communicated and had dealings with him fifty years ago."

2. "They have noticias of Doña Madalena de Mendoza and Ruy Diaz de Mendoza, el viejo, and Doña Catalina de Salazar, maternal grandparents."

3. "They heard that Doña Catalina de Salazar and Ruy Diaz de Mendoza, el viejo, were married in the indias, where she was widowed and then married Captain Cristobal de Oñate in Mexico."

4. "Doña Madalena, mother of the candidate, was from the mother side and sister to Adelantado Don Juan de Oñate."

5. "They sold a hacienda of Doña Catalinas from this jurisdiction in Belicena."

6. "They are caballeros, hijodalgos notorios de sangre."

7. "Ruy Diaz de Mendoza, brother to the mother of the candidate, was estimated by all that the Marqueses de Mondejar treated him like a duedo."

8. "Doña Mayor de Castro, widow of the deceased Juan Mendoza, said that he was the first cousin of Ruy Diaz de Mendoza, el viejo, the uncle of Madalena, mother of the candidate, she (Mayor de Castro) is a person who is principal and is credible."

9. "Ruy Diaz de Mendoza, brother of the candidate's mother, was veinticuatro of this city in 1579."

On the fourth of October of the same year. Juan Alvares de la Vega, vecino and natural of Granada:

1. "He knows by having heard and seen the papers

that Ruy Diaz de Mendoza and Doña Catalina Salazar, naturals of this city of Granada, were maternal grandparents of Vicente Mendoza."

2. "She was the the maternal sister of Don Juan Oñate, Adelantado de New Mexico."

3. "Doña Catalina in her second marriage to Cristobal de Oñate".

4. Vicente Zaldivar, the candidate, is the nephew Juan de Onate."

5. "Ruy Diaz de Mendoza, maternal grandfather of the candidate, was a relative of de los Marqueses de Mondejar. In particular, he heard from Gabriel Maldonado … de cabildo of Granada that this is true."

6. "He knew in the city that Ruy Diaz de Mendoza, veinticuatro and a brother of his named Cristobal de Oñate came from the Indias and went to Belicena. A place where they had many haciendas and with them was their uncle Agustin de Salazar, clerigo."

7. "He saw them at the place of Sancho de Castro, beneficiado of that town, now deceased."

8. "He had known a sister named Madalena de Mendoza who was married in the Indias. Her parents were named Ruy Diaz de Mendoza and Doña Catalina de Salazar, naturales of the city of Granada.

9. "He heard from his parents and elders from Belicena, where they had a hacienda, that the Oñates and Mendozas were powerful people from the Indias."

10. "Ruy Diaz de Mendoza lived in this city and was the son of Ruy diaz de Mendoza and Doña Catalina Salazar. They were caballeros hijosdalgo."

In the same year and month. Gabriel Maldonado, portero de Cabildo de la cuidad de Granada, vecino and natural.

1. "He has noticias of Doña Madalena de Mendoza, his mother, because more than fifty years ago he knew Ruy Diaz de Mendoza, veinticuatro, her brother."

2. "He knew their parents Ruy Diaz de Mendoza and Doña Catalina de Salazar, naturals of Granada, they were married in the Indias where Doña Catalina was widowed."

In the City of Granada. Don Fernando Alvares de Zapata, Señor de las villas de las Guajaras:

1. "Ruy Diaz de Mendoza, who he knew, was a caballero muy principal. He was procurador de cortes of this city and his majesty granted him the tesorero of the Casa de Moneda in Mexico."

In the same city. Doña Mayor de Castro, vecina and natural of this city of Granada:

1. "She was married to Juan Mendoza, vecino of this city, uncle of Madalena de Mendoza, mother of the candidate and of Ruy Diaz de Mendoza, veinticuatro, who was of this city, and first cousin of Ruy Diaz de Mendoza, his father. Juan Mendoza, my husband, in letters the said Doña Madalena Mendoza treated him like an uncle of hers. I have noticias the the parents of Doña Madelena were named Ruy Diaz de Mendoza and Doña Catalina de Salazar, daughter of Gonzalo de Salazar, and naturals of the city of Granada. Likewise, they were caballeros, hijodalgos notorios de sangre according to the fueros and customs of

Spain. Luis Hurtado de Mendoza was of the Abito de Alcantara, Juan Mendoza, father of the above mentioned, was given the Santiago; Don Rodrigo de la Cerda, caballero of the city of Cordoba, was habito de Alcantara and second cousin to the mother of the candidate; Don Luis Carrillo de Carvajal was Abito de Santiago and grandson of Juan Mendoza, my husband. Doña Ynes, daughter of my said husband, was given the Abito de Santiago. They are duedos of the Marqueses de Mondejar y muy grande caballeros y illustres."

According to Jose Antonio Esquibel there was not enough information to discover Ruy Diaz Mendoza's ancestors. He created a chart showing some of the relationships. This is my chart showing the same relationships as Esquibel.

Juan Mendoza Mayor de Castro	**first cousins**	**Ruy Diaz Mendoza** Catalina Salazar
Ines Mendoza	*X Mendoza*	Vicente Zaldivar Madalena Mendoza
	Luis Carrillo	Madalena Mendoza Juan Guerra Resa

3 RE EVALUATION/METHODS

Is there really no more information to be had from these testimonies? What is important about Ruy Diaz Mendoza?

1. He was a caballero hijodalgo.
2. He was a duedo of the Marqueses de Mondejar.
3. He died in the Indias.
4. He was from Granada or Baeza.
5. Ruy Diaz Mendoza II was a veinticuatro. He had to be noble to hold office. A limpieza de sangre was required.
6. A hacienda in Belicena was owned by Catalina.
7. Agustin Salazar was an uncle.
8. Juan Mendoza, first cousin to Ruy Diaz Mendoza, was married to Mayor de Castro.
9. Don Rodrigo de la Cerda was a second cousin of Madalena.
10. Luis Carrillo was a second cousin of Madalena. He was also a step grandson to Doña Mayor de Castro. He had the habito de Santiago.
11. Juan de Mendoza a caballero de Orden de Santiago.
12. Juan de Mendoza, husband of Mayor Castro, was an uncle of Madalena.
13. Luis Hurtado de Mendoza granted the Santiago to Juan de Mendoza.

Actually, there is enough information to solve the case. Due to lack of punctuation it is easy to lose context of what is being said. Doña Mayor de Castro's original statement in spanish:

1. "Recibimos juramento en la forma acostumbrada de doña Mayor de Castro, vecina y natural de esta ciudad de Granada la qual prometio de bajo del decir verdad y guardar siento y es edad de mas de setenta años y siendo preguntada por las preguntas de interrogato dijo: que tuvo casada con Juan de Mendoza vecino que fue de esta cuidad tio de Doña Madalena de Mendoza madre del pretendiente y de Rui Diaz de Mendoza vienticuatro que fue de esta cuidad y primo hermano de Rui Dias de Mendoza su padre que en esto le tocan las generales pero que no por hecho dejara de decir la verdad de lo que se la a preguntado y asi debajo del juramento hecho dijo que tiene noticia de doña Madalena Mendoza la qual fue casada in las indias con Vicente de Zaldivar caballero Vizcaino y que la dicha doña Madalena vio muchas cartas escritas a Rui Diaz de Mendoza her brother veinticuatro que fue de estas cuidad. Y que el dicho Juan Mendoza su marido se trava con la dicha doña Madalena por cartas como tio suyo y tambian tiene noticia de que los pas de dicha doña Madalena de llamaba Rui Dias de Mendoza y doña Catalina de Salazar hija de Gonzalo de Salazar naturales de la ciudad de Granada y que por las razones...tiene la noticias que tiene referida del pretendiente y su madre y abuelos maternos y sabe mas que la dicha doña Catalina Salazar fue casada de segundo matrimonio en las indias con el capitan Cristobal de Oñate y que un hijo suyo llamaba don Alonso de Oñate le visito a este declarante el ano de seiscientos el qual

vino de las indias a tomar que tad y disponer de una hacienda que tenia en Belicena y asi eran hermanos de la parte de madre de dicho Don Alonso y sus hermanos, y sus juramentos decia dicha doña Madalena madre del pretendiente y de Ruy Diaz veinticuatro que fue de esta ciudad al cual comunico y trato como sobrino del dicho marido y avi esta declarante se acuerda de haberse enganado (?) mucho por causa de la persuasion que le queria estima y por el conocimiento que tiene..y asimismo fueron caballeros hijosdalgos notorios de sangre segun fuero y costumbre de espana y christianos viejos limpios de toda mala raza todos nombrados y sus ascendientes en confirmacion de lo qual dijo que comendador Luis Hurtado de Mendoza fue del abito de Alcantara y Juan de Mendoza padre del susodicho se le dieron de santiago y don Rodrigo de la Cerda caballero de la ciudad de Cordova es del abito del Alcantara primo segundo de la madre de la pretendiente y que Don Luis Carrillo de Carvajal del Abito de Santiago es nieto de Juan Mendoza marido que fue de este testigo y Doña Ynes hija del dicho su marido le dieron el Abito de Santiago haciendo los informaciones como caballero porque sasad lo tuvo estos primos y tios de la dicha doña Madalena madre del pretendiente u en esta familia otros muchos abitos que esta declarante no se aquerda estan notoria la nobleza y limpieza los contenidos que no hay nadie que puede con verdad decir lo contrario y asimismo dijo que los dichos so duedos de los Marqueses de Mondejar que no sabe y aido que ninguno de los nombrados ni de sus ascendientes hayan sido castigados ni penitencia los por el santo oficio no infamados por otra justicia que todos han sido muy grandes caballeros y este muy ilustre.. Doña Mayor Castro, firmo

The most crucial evidence from all the testimonies given is Doña Mayor de Castro's last two hundred words. She gives the name of the father of Ruy Diaz de Mendoza as Juan de Mendoza, caballero de Orden de Santiago. Juan de Mendoza, Caballero de la Orden de Santiago, was wrongly identified as the father of Doña Mayor de Castro's husband Juan de Mendoza by Esquibel. The distinction is made by the words she uses. El dicho is used twice to refer to her husband. El susodicho refers to the subject Ruy Diaz de Mendoza.

Next Step: Researching Belicena records may uncover new documents.

4 BELICENA

Belicena is a small town close to the city of Granada. So small, it wasn't a town during Mendoza's time and there was no kept archives for the early 16th century. This means that Belicena was under another jurisdiction. The closest town to Belicena is Santa Fe. There is an archive for Santa Fe, Granada for the 16th century. There are available Mendoza extractions up to 1550 and anything that might be relevant: Analysis in bold print.

First appearance of Ruy Diaz de Mendoza
1543, January, 30. Belicena.
Ruy Diaz de Mendoza, Catalina de Salazar, his wife and
for Gonzalo de Salazar, her father, gives lease to Alonso Muzmudi and Isabel Muzmudi, Francisco el Gaviari and Catalina Gaviaria, vecinos of Belicena, a plot of land to build two houses, for 14 reales and 2 gallinas for the year.
Protocolo Juan de Barrionuevo, V II
Fols.12v-16v/203v-207v/v.
Catalog Number: 788

1544, August, 31. Sante Fe.
Testament.
Catalina Perez de Muros, vecina de Santa Fe, widow of Juan

Rajadel.
1. Rents with a Mendoza, a son in law of Juan Alvares, vecino of Granada.
2. A debt with Juan Hurtado de Mendoza.

Protocolo de Diego Ruiz, VII
Fols. 225r-231v. /753-759v/.
Catalog Number: 1250
1515, October, 25.
Escritura de compraventa de vina y tierras otorgada con poder.
P.F.O.I.; fol./3r/v/.
Juan De Segovie, vecino of Santa Fe, in the name of Bacheller Nicasio de Linan, vicario y beneficiado de Loja, by his power that continues here:
1. "By the power of the said, he sells Juan de Mendoza, vecino de Granada, a vineyard de 5 marjales, at the edge of Santa Fe, next to the vineyard of Juana Dominguez."

1515, October, 24.
Escritura de obligación de pago por compraventa de vinas y tierras.
P.F.O.I.; fols. /5v-6r/.
Juan de Mendoza, vecino of Granada, escudero, que es de las...y criado del Señor Marques Don Luis de Mendoza, he is obliged to a pay Bachiller Nicassio de Linan, beneficiado y vicario de Loja, 9970 maravedis, for lands and vineyards he bought; to be paid before the Easter of 1516.
Analysis:
1. **A knight in training is an escudero.**
2. **This is consistent with Mayor de Castro testimony that Don Luis de Mendoza granted to Juan de Mendoza the habit of order of Santiago. Juan could not receive entry without training. This Juan Mendoza is Ruy Diaz de Mendoza's father.**

3.   Is there more than one Juan Mendoza in the service as an escudero? Unlikely.

1515, October, 24.
Escritura de ratificacion.
P.F.O.I.; fol./6v/.
Ana de Negral, wife of Juan de Mendoza, criado del Señor Marques de Valhermoso, affirms the barter her husband made with Martin Lopez and Maria de Linares, his wife. Before Ruy Lopez de la Puente, escribano publico de Santa Fe, 25 de enero de 1515, 39 marjales of land in the villa in two pieces.
Analysis:
1.   **Ana Negral is the wife of Juan Mendoza.**
2.   **Marques de Mondejar holds Valhermoso.**
3.   **Juan de Mendoza and Ana de Negral fit the timeline and the fact of being in Belicena and Granada, Spain. Too coincidental not be his parents.**

1516, Abril, 17.
P.F.O.I.; fol. 118r/v./74r/v/.
Escritura de olbigacion de pago por compraventa de animal. Mention of Andres de Negral, Alcaide de la Villa.

1520. s.m.s.d.
P.F.O.I.; fols. 344v-345r./306v-307r/.
Juan al Gazi mentions Captain Juan Hurtado de Mendoza.
Further research of Juan Hurtado is that he is the husband of Mencia Santaren.

1520. January, 29.
P.F.O.I.; 340v-341r./302v-303r/.
Escritura de arrendamiento de tierras.
Juan de Mendoza, Alguacil de la Malaha and vecino de Padul.

1520. July, 20.

P.F.O.I.; fol.401r/v/372r/v/.
Escritura de aparceria de tierras.
The captain Juan Hurtado de Mendoza, vecino de Granada.

1521, May, 15.
P.F.O.I.; fols. 257v./217v/.
Escritura de poder especial para cobrar y general para pleitos.
Francisco Negral, Alcaide and vecino of Sante Fe.
Analysis:
Ana Negral probably related to Francisco Negral and Andres Negral.

1542, Junio, 25.
PDRIV.; fols. 299v-300v./577v-578r/.
Escritura de poder especial para cobrar.
Ruy Diaz de Mendoza, vecino of Granada, gives authority to Gonzalo de Cuevas, vecino of Granada.
Witness: Juan Mendoza, vecino of Sante Fe.

Belicena, 1543. Enero, 30.
P.J.B.II.; fols. 12v-16v./203v-207r/v/.
Escritura de constitucion de censo reservativo sobre solar.
Ruy Diaz de Mendoza and Catalina de Salazar, his wife, vecinos de Belicena, jurisdiction de Granada, in name of Gonzalo de Salazar, my father and father in law, give perpetual lease to Alonso Muzmudi.

Belicena, 1543, Enero, 30.
P.J.B.II.; fols. 16v-206.
Escritura de constitucion de censo reservativo sobre casa (solar).
Ruy Diaz de Mendoza and Catalina de Salazar, his wife, vecinos de Belicena, limits of Granada, gives perpetual lease to Miguel Copaz and Isabel Copaz.

Belicena, 1544, Enero, 27.
P.J.B.II.; fols. 210r-214r./377r-381r/.
Escritura de constitucion de censo reservativo sobre tierra.
Ruy Diaz de Mendoza and Catalina de Salazar, his wife,
vecinos de Belicena, jurisdiction of Granada, in the name of
Señor Gonzalo de Salazar, father, gives perpetual lease to
Alonso Garcia and Leonor Garcia.
Witness: Garcia de Mendoza, vecino of Santa Fe.

1544, April, 9.
PJBII.; fol.233v./400v/.
Escritura de obligacion de pago por compraventa de grano.
Unknown, vecino de Santa Fe, pays Ruy Diaz de Mendoza,
vecino de Belicena, jurisdiction de Granada, 56 reales for 8
bushels of wheat, for 7 reales, to be paid August 1.

1544, Abril, 16.
P.J.B.II.; fol. 2366./403r/.
Escritura de obligacion de pago por compraventa de grano.
Gonzalo de Mendoza, vecino of Santa Fe, pays Ruy Diaz de
Mendoza, vecino of Belicena, jurisdiction of Granada, 21
reales for 3 bushels of wheat, to be paid August 1.

1544, Abril, 23.
P.J.B.II.; fol. 237r./404r/.
Escritura de obligacion de pago por compraventa de grano.
Pedro de Arevalo, vecino of Sante Fe, pays Ruy Diaz de
Mendoza, inhabitant in Belicena, jurisdiction of Granada 35
reales fors 5 bushels of wheat he bought.
Witness: Garcia de Mendoza.

1544. April, 30.
P.J.B.II.; fol. 239v./406v/.
Escritura de obligacion de pago por compraventa de grano.

Hernan Martin, vecino de Santa Fe, pays Ruy Diaz de Mendoza, vecino de Belicena, 42 reales for 6 bushels of wheat, to be paid on Santa Maria de Agosto (August 15)

Escribano: Juan de Barrionuevo
1544, Mayo, 12.
P.J.B.II.; fol.253r./420r/.
Escritura de obligacion de pago por compraventa de grano. Juan Gonzalez de Toledo, vecino de Santa Fe, pays Ruy Diaz de Mendoza, vecino of Belicena, 28 reales for 4 bushels of wheat and 14 reales for 2 bushels, a prior obligation, on 1, August.

Margins: 22, Febrero, 1545.
Ruy Diaz de Mendoza releases Juan Gonzales from the 28 reales obligation.
Signed: Ruy Diaz de Mendoza
Escribano: Juan de Barrionuevo
Analysis:
1. Ruy Diaz Mendoza left for New Spain after February 1545.
2. He didn't leave with Viceroy Antonio de Mendoza but by request of him. Antonio Mendoza left nearly ten years earlier.

1546, Julio, 22.
P.D.R.III.; fol. 230r./324r/.
Escritura de poder especial para cobrar.
Juan de Mendoza, vecino de Alhambra de la ciudad de Granada, gives authority to Ines Farfana, his mother and Sebastian de Coca, brother in law.

1546, Octubre, 9
P.D.R.III.; fols. 313v-316r./69v-72r/.
Ines de Farfana, widow of Diego de Mendoza, vecina of Santa Fe, with Geronimo de Mendoza, vecino de Baeza; Juan de Mendoza, her sons; for Diego de Mendoza, her son; ratify, sell

to Sebastian de Coca and Doña Leonor Mendoza his wife, two houses. Two pieces of vineyard next to Juan Mendoza, deceased.

Signed: Ines Farfana, Juan Mendoza, Geronimo Mendoza.

1546, October, 9.
P.D.R.III.; fol. 319r/v./75r/v/.

Ines Farfana, widow of Diego de Mendoza, vecina de Santa Fe, gives authority to Leonor Farfana, her mother, vecina de Granada, to collect from Sebastian de Coca and Leonor Mendoza, vecinos of Santa Fe.

Escribano: Diego Ruiz

Analysis:
1. Could be relatives of Ruy Diaz de Mendoza.
2. Ana Negral was probably related to a conquistador of Granada name Diego de Negral, the son of Pedro Gutierrez de Negral and Maria de la Carcel. Diego was married to Teresa de Cuello. This family were hijosdalgos from Fontiveros, Avila, Spain.

Survey Book of Belicena 1570-1572

1. Cristobal de Onate, vecino de Belicena, cristiano viejo, administer of the hacienda de Agustin de Salazar, 2 houses together, next to Sancho de Castro and other next to Juan el Modon u the
2. Ruy Diaz de Mendoza, veinticuatro de Granada, no house.
3. Casa principal de Ruy Diaz de Mendoza, old christian.

Analysis: This is consistent with the information in the earlier testimonies.

Next step: Reconstructing.

5 NEW EVIDENCE 1

A reconstructed family tree of Ruy Diaz de Mendoza may be possible with the evidence provided by Doña Mayor de Castro. Doña Mayor de Castro stated:

"Rodrigo de la Cerda, caballero de la cuidad de Cordova, es del Abito de Alcantara, primo segundo de la madre de pretendiente..."

Obviously, in english, "Rodrigo de la Cerda is a caballero from the city of Cordoba, and a member of the order of Alcantara, second cousin to the mother of the candidate."

Mendoza	Mendoza
x	Ruy Diaz de Mendoza
Rodrigo de la Cerda	Madalena Mendoza
	Vicente Zaldivar

There is no application of Rodrigo de la Cerda's entry into the Alcantara order. In the chart above, the common relationship Rodrigo de la Cerda and Magdalena Mendoza is a Mendoza. Rodrigo and Magdalena have the same great paternal ancestor. There is no way to determine their common Mendoza ancestor directly without Rodrigo de la Cerda's birth church record or limpieza de sangre from the order of Alcantara.

There is still a way to figure out their common ancestor. What if Rodrigo de la Cerda had children or descendants who joined one of the several military orders? Sometimes the limpieza de sangres identified ancestors beyond the grandparents. A search of surnames and locations is way to parse out possible relatives of Rodrigo de la Cerda. The search resulted the application of Juan Ceron de la Cerda into the Order of Santiago. July 14, 1614.

Juan Ceron de la Cerda
Parents:
Martin Ceron de Benavides, Caballero de Calatrava, 24 of Jaen
&
Doña Beatris de la Cerda y Mendoza, natural of Baeza
Paternal Grandparents:
Juan Ceron, vecino y natural of Jaen and 24
&
Doña Mariana Contreras y Benavides, natural of Jaen
Maternal Grandparents:
Fernando de la Cerda, Señor de la Vega, natural of Cordoba &
Doña Marina de la Mendoza, natural of Baeza

In the city of Baeza on the nineteenth day of the same month and year..Don Rodrigo Nicuesa y Mendoza, commissioner of the Santo Officio..he receives oath.

1.   "He states he knows the said Don Juan Ceron de la

Cerda, the candidate...and that he has known him for 18 years. He knows where he was born and knows he was the legitimate son of Martin Ceron de Benavides and Doña Beatris de la Cerda y Mendoza. He has known them for over 30 years and that he possessed the habit of the order of Calatrava. And knows he was born in the said city, the said Don Martin Ceron. The said Doña Beatris de la Cerda, his wife, was from the parish of Salvador of the said city. The said Martin Ceron, the father, was a vecino and natural of the city of Jaen...and that he knew Don Fernando de la Cerda and Doña Marina de Mendoza, the maternal grandparents of the said Don Juan Ceron de la Cerda, the candidate. He knows the said Don Fernando was a natural of Cordoba and the said Doña Marina de Mendoza was from the city of Baeza. Everyone knows this for it is public knowledge"

2. " One of witness' sisters is married to the great-grandparent of Don Juan, the candidate."

3. "He knows that Juan Ceron de la Cerda, candidate, and the others he knows are caballeros, nobles, and hijosdalgos according to the fueros of Spain. They are not moors, jews, conversos in any grade. He knows Martin Ceron, his father, is a familiar del Santo Officio and is presently has the habito de Calatrava and the same of Rodrigo de la Cerda, tio hermano of the said Doña Beatris, his mother...and is Familar de Santo Officio.

4. "He says the grandmother, of the said, her name is Doña Marina de Mendoza, she was natural of the city of Baeza...she is clean, an old christian, noble and proven; for it is public and well-known."

5. "Martin Ceron, his father, served his Majesty in the Galleys of Spain.

Analysis: The statement above verifies that the Rodrigo de la Cerda is the same man Mayor de Castro and Rodrigo Nicuesa mentions in their testimony. Also:

1. Rodrigo's father is from Cordoba.
2. He is a caballero.
3. He is hijodalgo.
4. He is a relative to a Mendoza.
5. Marina Mendoza is the mother of Rodrigo de la Cerda and Beatris de la Cerda.
6. Marina Mendoza was from the parish of Salvador in Baeza.

The only confusion is which order Rodrigo de la Cerda belonged to. He may have belonged to both orders. The rebuilding of the family line now starts with Marina de Mendoza as the mother of Rodrigo de la Cerda and Beatris de la Cerda. The fathers of Marina de la Cerda and Ruy Diaz de Mendoza are siblings.

x mendoza	x mendoza
Fernando de la Cerda & **Marina Mendoza**	Ruy Diaz de Mendoza
Martin Ceron & Beatris de la Cerda sister to **Rodrigo de la Cerda**	Magdalena de Mendoza
Juan Ceron Cerda	Vicente de Zaldivar

Juan de Parraga, veinticuatro , more than 40 years old.

1. "He said he knows said Don Juan Ceron de la Cerda, the candidate, for 20 years, for he was born in Jaen in the house of his parents, who are named Don Martin Ceron and Doña Beatris de la Cerda y Mendoza. He knows this by the noticias of the said Don Martin, that his father is a natural of Jaen and Doña Beatris is a natural of this city. He knows Don Fernando de la Cerda y Mendoza and Doña Marina de Mendoza, paternal grandparents of said candidate. He knows the said Fernando was called Mendoza because in his marriage contract to Doña Mariana, he was named Mendoza. He knows this because he seen the contract. He knows that Doña Beatris de la Cerda y Mendoza is a natural of this city, the same as Doña Marina Mendoza."

2. "Don Martin Ceron, his father, has the Habito de Calatrava. So did a legitimate brother of the said Doña Beatris, his wife. His name was Rodrigo de la Cerda y Mendoza and he had the Habito de Calatrava. He knows both the father and uncle are Familiares del Santo Officio.

3. "Doña Marina de Mendoza, maternal grandmother of said candidate, was a natural of the this city. She was noble and "muy principal."

In the city of Baeza, on the 8th day of the same month and year. Alonso Leguga, vecino and natural of this city.

1. "He does not know Don Juan Ceron, the candidate. He has known his father for over 30 years. His name was Don Martin Ceron and Beatris de la Cerda. He knows Doña Beatris de la Cerda was a natural of this city. He knows her parents. Their names were Don Fernando de la Cerda and Doña Marina de Mendoza, maternal grandparents

of Don Juan."

2. "Don Juan Ceron, the candidate, his parents and maternal grandparents were legitimate and naturals of their parents."

3. "Don Juan, parents, and grandparents have always been caballeros, nobles, and hijosdalgo according to the fueros of Spain.

4. "Doña Marina, natural of this city, clean and old christian. She is very noble. A daughter of caballeros, very noble of this city."

In the city of Baeza, on the 8th day of the same year. Doctor Don Hernando de Pedraza, Prior of the church of Salvador in this city.

1. "He does not know Juan de Ceron the candidate. He knows his parents and maternal grandparents. Their names are Don Fernando de la Cerda and Doña Marina de Mendoza and Don Martin Ceron and Doña Beatris de la Cerda. He knows that Doña Marina de Mendoza and Doña Beatris de la Cerda, mother, maternal grandmother of the candidate, were naturals of this city."

In the city on the 8th day of the same month and year. Baltasar Serrano de San Juan, natural of this city.

1. "He does not know Don Juan Ceron de la Cerda, the candidate. He knew Don Martin Ceron and Doña Beatris de la Cerda, his parents. He knew Don Fernando de la Cerda and Marina de Mendoza, maternal grandparents of the candidate Don Juan. He knows Doña Beatris de la Cerda, mother of Don Juan, is a natural of this city. Doña Marina de Mendoza, his maternal grandmother, is as well. He knows this because Doña Beatris de la

Cerda and Don Martin Ceron married here. He came from Jaen. Doña Marina, her mother, was the daughter of Geronimo de Mendoza. During his marriage (Geronimo) he procreated his legitimate and natural daughter Doña Marina, legitimate wife of Don Fernando. He was a natural of Cordoba. During the marriage of Don Fernando de la Cerda and Doña Marina de Mendoza they had a legitimate daughter named Beatris de la Cerda, wife of Martin Ceron. Both are parents of the candidate. They had homes in this city.

2. "They all were legitimate and natural children of their parents."

3. "He knows Don Rodrigo de la Cerda, brother to the parents and brother to Doña Beatris, also had the Habito to Calatrava. He is also Familiar del Santo Officio de la Inquisition in the… and city of Cordoba."

Analysis:

1. Geronimo de Mendoza was the father of Marina de Mendoza.

2. The Mendozas were from the parish of Salvador in Baeza.

3. Don Rodrigo de la Cerda lived in Cordoba and held office.

4. Beatris de la Cerda and Rodrigo are second cousins to Madalena Mendoza.

5. Geronimo is the uncle of Ruy Diaz de Mendoza.

Geronimo Mendoza	x Mendoza
Marina Mendoza & Fernando de la Cerda	Ruy Diaz de Mendoza
Beatris de la Cerda & Martin Ceron	Madalena Mendoza
Juan de la Cerda	Vicente Zaldivar

Next Step: Do cursory research on Rodrigo de la Cerda and Martin Ceron. I was able to find corroborating evidence.

Evidence I:
Memorial de Martin Ceron de Benavides, Procurador por Jaen.

"With my brothers, duedos, ancestors; and those of Beatris de la Cerda, my wife, served in the same manner during times of peace and war. The grandfather of doña Beatris de la Cerda served as captain in Italy and other parts of the empire of our lord. Her grandfather served in the war of Pavia. Jeronimo de Mendoza served some years in the corregimiento in the city of Avila."
Note: The war of Pavia 1521-1525.

Corresponding evidence II:
Señor Don Rodrigo de la Cerda Mendoza, limpieza de sangre for veinticuatro. Cordoba April 28, 1608. Diego de Aguayo y Godoy, caballero de Calatrava and veinticuatro.
1. "He knows Don Rodrigo de la Cerda y Mendoza, caballero de Abito de Calatrava. He knew Don

Fernando de la Cerda and Doña Marina de Mendoza, his wife; father and mother of Rodrigo de la Cerda. Both are deceased. He knew Geronimo de Mendoza and Doña Catalina Mendoza, his wife; father and mother of Marina de Mendoza. Don Rodrigo de la Cerda is the legitimate son of Don Fernando de la Cerda and Doña Marina de Mendoza, his wife. They are caballeros and hijosdalgos notorios de sangre and calidad.

Analysis:
1. Catalina Mendoza was the wife of Geronimo de Mendoza.
2. Catalina and Geronimo were the parents of Marina.
3. Don Rodrigo de la Cerda's limpieza de sangre corroborates with the same information as Juan de la Cerda's limpieza de sangre.

6 New Evidence 2

A second search for family names resulted in Luis de Carvajal's application in 1588 for the Order of Santiago. These papers were difficult to read.

Don Luis de Carvajal, natural de Baeza
Parents:
Cristobal de Carvajal & Doña Isabel Ana de Mendoza
Paternal Grandparents:
Luis Carrillo de Carvajal & Doña Catalina Aranda, natural of Alcala la Real
Maternal Grandparents:
Juan de Mendoza & Doña Maria de Carvajal, both from Baeza

First Witness:
1. "He knows Juan Mendoza and he does not know whose son he is. He knew him in Granada and he was in the service of the Marques de Mondejar. I don't know the name of his parents and where they were from."

Geronimo Garico:
1. "He knew Juan Mendoza, son in law of Alonso de Carvajal. The father of the said was Luis de Mendoza. They are naturals and nobles of this

place. He left a widow. Her name is Doña Fulana
de Farfana. They were married in the court of
Granada. A habito of Santiago was granted to a
daughter of Juan de Mendoza, the sister of the
mother of Luis de Carvajal. Luis de Mendoza, the
father of Juan Mendoza, was a natural of the city.
He was married in Granada with Fulana Farfana.
Juan Mendoza was born in Granada."
Fulana means unknown.

Analysis:

1. Juan Mendoza was born in Granada.
2. Luis Mendoza and Fulana Farfana, who we know
   as Ynes Farfana, are the parents of Juan de
   Mendoza. This information is consistent with the
   Belicina information. They are cousins to Ruy Diaz
   de Mendoza
3. Luis de Mendoza and Geronimo de Mendoza are
   brothers.
4. Luis de Mendoza full name is Diego Luis Mendoza.
5. Don Alonso de Carvajal is the father in law of Juan
   Mendoza.

Diego Luis Mendoza	Juan Mendoza	Geronimo Mendoza
Juan Mendoza	Ruy Mendoza	Marina Mendoza
Isabel Ana	Madalena	Beatris and Rodrigo Cerda

Rodrigo de Mendoza, vecino of this city and regidor:

1. "He knows Juan Mendoza. Juan Mendoza was
   born in Granada. He does not know his parents.
   He heard his name was Diego de Mendoza and his
   wife was named Ynes de Farfana. She was from the

corte de Seville. He heard this from his wife Ana Mogia."

2. "The are very clean and ancient hijosdalgos. In this city the Habito de Santiago was granted to the daughter of Juan Mendoza, who is in Granada."

Analysis: The daughter of Juan de Mendoza received the Habito de Santiago. This is consistent of Mayor de Castro's testimony. Diego Luis Mendoza never received the Habito or it would have been mentioned by the witnesses. Again, Mayor de Castro was referring to Juan de Mendoza as the father of Ruy Diaz de Mendoza, not her husband.

Juan de Benavides Mesia, vecino:
1. "He does not know Don Luis Carvajal. He knew Cristobal de Carvajal and Doña Isabel Ana de Mendoza. They are the parents of Don Luis. They were vecinos. He knows Luis Carrillo Carvajal and Doña Catalina de Aranda, parents of Don Cristobal Carvajal. Catalina de Aranda was from Alcala."

Don de Avalos, resident of Baeza:
1. "He knows Don Cristobal de Carvajal and Doña Isabel Ana Mendoza, parents of Don Luis. He knew Juan Mendoza and doña Maria de Carvajal, parents of Isabel Ana de Mendoza. He understands Juan de Mendoza was from Granada."

Analysis: Juan Mendoza's first wife was Maria de Carvajal. He then married Mayor de Castro. This confirms Mayor de Castro's testimony that Luis Carrillo y Carvajal was the grandson of her husband Juan de Mendoza.

Francisco Corbera, vecino:

1. "He knew Juan de Mendoza. He was a duedo of el Marques de Mondejar. His parents he did not know who or where they were from."

Diego Robles:
1. "He knew Juan de Mendoza, very well. He did not know his parents because they lived in Granada. They were duedos or relatives of the casa de Marques de Mondejar."

Catalina de Mendoza, widow of Don Geronimo Mendoza:
1. "She knew Juan de Mendoza, maternal grandfather of said Don Luis. She knew Diego de Mendoza and Ynes de Farfana, his wife. They were the parents of Juan Mendoza and great grandparents of Don Luis. They were naturales of this city (Baeza). Ruy Diaz de Mendoza, father in law of the the witness, went to Granada to stay with el Marquis de Mondejar. Diego de Mendoza was camarero of the Marques de Mondejar. The Mendozas knew them very well."

Analysis:
1. Ruy Diaz de Mendoza is the grandfather of Ruy Diaz de Mendoza.
2. Diego de Mendoza and Geronimo are the sons of Ruy Diaz de Mendoza. Neither of them had the habito of any order because that would have been mentioned. Again, Juan de Mendoza is the father of Ruy Diaz de Mendoza.
3. Luis Carrillo Carvajal, the candidate, is the second cousin to Madalena Mendoza. This confirms Mayor de Castro's testimony.
4. Mexia surname is a mistake for Ruy Diaz Mendoza. None of his descendants carried the name or mention it. He also had no descendants living in

Baeza. The witness from Francisco Rivadeneira's interrogation did not know Ruy Diaz de Mendoza, but probably knew of Geronimo's descendants who married a Mexia Cerda. They were more prominent and lived in Baeza.

	Ruy Diaz Mendoza	
Diego Mendoza	Juan Mendoza	Geronimo Mendoza
Isabel	Ruy Diaz Mendoza	Marina
Luis Carrillo	Madalena Mendoza	Rodrigo Cerda

7 MENDOZA FAMILY

The following information was the final part of the investigation on Ruy Diaz de Mendoza's paternal line. Originally, I read Gonzalo Argote de Molina's *Nobleza del Andaluzia,* to study the people and history of Baeza, Jaen. Argote's book is considered a resource by historians and genealogist because of his accuracy. The information was helpful, but there was no person to connect the information with at the time. I decided to review the information again. To hold any public office an official had to be of noble blood. Geronimo de Mendoza provided his lineage which was recorded by Gonzalo Argote de Molina. I found that the Argote's information was consistent with other material he wasn't aware of at the time. This is what he wrote:

"Juan de Mendoza, who died in the battle of Linuesa. His lineage and Arms. Cap CX. From the letters who Geronimo de Mendoza, regidor de Baeza, Mayorazgo y Caballero de los mas principales of this city, they showed me his lineage and that I saw the papers and in the writings of the time, this is very faithful and true. Juan de Mendoza, who died in the battle of Linuesa, was the son of Ruy Diaz de Mendoza and Leonor Alonso de Godoy. She was the daughter of Pero Alonso de Godoy and this Juan Mendoza was married to the daughter of Sancho Garcia de Cardenas, Regidor of Baeza, de los mas ricos y principales de Caballeros. Sancho Garcia Cardenas had no male descendants, only daughters. The oldest daughter Sancha Garcia de Cardenas married Ruy Fernandez de Fuenmayor. The second, Juana Garcia de Cardenas, married this Caballero. They had a son named Luis Lopez de Mendoza, who was Justicia Mayor of Baeza for Constable Ruy Lopez de Davalos. He had a son Juan de Mendoza, the Regidor de Baeza and the Comendador de Villahermosa of the Order of Santiago, who the Moors murdered in a fight at los Vado de las Carretas. Whose succession is continued in this book, which the Mayorazgo y Casa was succeeded by Don Fernando de la Cerda, el Mayorazgo principal de Cordoba. They are the Caballeros del Prestamero mayor de Vizcaya and whose Arms were "banda verde con Perfiles de oro campo roxo" first Arms of this lineage and from the Cadenas in the battle of Las Navas de Tolosa, which was won by the ancestor of these Caballeros."

Rodrigo de Mendoza and Leonor Alonso de Godoy
Juan de Mendoza and Sancha Garcia Cardenas
Luis Lopez de Mendoza
Juan de Mendoza
↓
Geronimo de Mendoza
Mayorazgo de Fernando de la Cerda

The rest of Ruy Diaz Mendoza's paternal lineage can be found in the book. In the section, *Alfonso de Carvajal VaSobre el Castillo de Linares, el qual le fue defendido por Gil Ramirez de Davalos y los de su linage. Cap. CCXXXIX,* the Mendoza line is mentioned:

"He was Rodrigo de Mendoza, son of Comendador Juan de Mendoza, who was memorialized in cap.110, he was married to Isabel Rodriguez de Peralta...they left an illustrious succession. The other children were doña Leonor de Mendoza, who was married to Alonso de Carvajal, Señor de Tovaruela." Leonor de Mendoza and her parents are mentioned in the limpieza de Sangre of Juan Carvajal.

Again the book continues:
" Alfonso Fernandez Valenzuela, Señor de Valenzuela, married in Baeza to the daughter of Rodrigo Narvaez Obispo de Jaen. Sancha Valenzuela married Rodrigo de Mendoza regidor de Baeza, y doña Aldonza de Sosa married Lope Ochoa de Cayzedo and Berenguela de Valenzuela, who married Regidor Martin de Zambrana."

In another document *Memorial de Zabrana,* written by the canon of Jaen, Gil Ramirez Davalos at the end of the 16th century, recorded the marriage of Rodrigo Mendoza with Doña Sancha Montemayor. This document was in the archivo of Enrique Toral Penaranda.

Year 1561. A plieto is entered by Fernando Cerda y Mendoza with Geronimo Mendoza to establish a mayorazgo. Argote statement is true.

Year 1559. In the limpieza de Sangre for Sancho Biedma Carvajal Valenzuela, Rodrigo Mendoza testified that the

Valenzuelas lived in the parish of Salvador in Baeza. The same parish as the Mendozas.

In 1345 Alfonso XI named the regidors, from a group of hijodalgos, as Alvar Iniguez de Narvaez and Sancho Garcia de Cardenas.

Rodrigo Mendoza	Leonor Godoy
Juan Mendoza	Sancha Garcia Cardenas
Luis Lopez Mendoza	
Juan Mendoza	Isabel Rodriguez Peralta
Rodrigo Mendoza	Sancha Valenzuela Montemayor
Rodrigo Mendoza	
Geronimo Mendoza	

8 Medina/Aranda

There was no wife named for Rodrigo de Mendoza. The only way to find possibly her name was to search randomly for information. I decided to search all the names listed as a witnesses in the previous limpieza de sangres for the Order of Santiago. The first name is Aranda and it is successful in providing the answer. This was luck. I was able to find two manuscripts for the years 1548 and 1741.

The following information is extracted from the noticias on the Aranda family for "Joachin de Aranda, caballero de Alcantara, Commendor de las Elges. Coronel de Regimiento de Dragones de Lusitiania, y Governador de Cartagena de Indias", completed by Sebastian Del Castillo Ruis de Molina, Cronista of the Kingdom, Rey de Armas de Rey. Certified in Madrid on June 19, 1741.

1. "Pedro Fernandez de Aranda, the first of the family, went to Alcala la Real to settle. He is a "principal" of the area. He married Juana Sanchez in the villa de Martos, daughter of Pasqual

Sanchez."

2. Pedro Fernandez is named in a cedula real by Rey
    Pedro: "Don Pedro, por the gracis de dios, Rey de
    Castilla, de León. Al concejo, Alcayde, e Alcaldes,
    Caballeros, Homes Buenos. que havedes deber
    facienda del dicho Concejo, Salud, e gracias, Bien
    Sabedes, como estan aca en mi servicio en esta
    guerra, que con el Rey de Aragón tengo, Gonzalo
    Fernandez de Cordova, Alcayde de Ayde esta villa,
    ocho homes de a cavallo, e porque a gran tiempo,
    que estan, e por bien se buelven, e ne su lugar
    vengan otros ocho, e los que havedes de embiar
    son Gonzalo Rodriguez, hijo de Rui Perez de
    Medina; Alfon Ruiz de Escamilla, el de a Cavallo,
    Pero Fernandez de Aranda, el Cavallo, Sancho
    Fernandez de Corbova, el de a Caballo; de Sevilla,
    el de a cavallo, Juan Fernandez de Terradillos, el de
    a Cavallo; Juan, hijo de Juan Perez de Ubeda, el de
    a Cavallo. Dada en Calatayud, sellada co mi sello de
    la Puridad 23. de Setiembre, era 1402. que es ando
    de Christo 1364."

3. "Pedro de Aranda and Juana de Sanchez had three
    children: Juan, Gonzalo, Andres, and Juana."

4. "Juana Sanchez de Aranda, the daughter of
    Pedro Fernandez de Aranda and Juana de Sanchez,
    married Pedro Gomez de Medina, Alcayde de
    Priego, son of Fernan Sanchez de Medina and
    Constanza Alvarez de Moya, grandson of Alvar
    Medina, Thesorero y Chanciller for King Alfonso
    XI.

5. "During their marriage they had two boy and girls:
    Luis and Pedro Medina; Doña Maria Diaz de
    Medina and Doña Juana de Medina.

6. "Luis de Medina, the oldest son, was Alcaide de

Priego. The Alcaide office was continued with his son Luis Gomez de Medina. Luis Gomez de Medina married Doña Catalina de Sotomayor, daughter of Gil Fernandez de Sotomayor and Doña Marina Fernandez Gadea. They had two children: Diego de Medina and Doña Maria de Medina y Aranda, who married in Baeza with Ruy Diaz de Mendoza. Their son Geronimo Mendoza was the maternal grandparent of Don Rodrigo de la Cerda, Señor de la Vega de Montoro, Caballero de orden Calatrava and veinticuatro de Cordova."

Analysis:

1. The last part of the testimony is consistent with Doña Mayor de Castro's testimony.

	Alvar de Medina
Pedro Aranda Juana Sanchez	Fernan Sanchez de Medina Constanza Alvarez de Moya
Juana Sanchez	Pedro Gomez Medina

Aranda Lina

Alvar de Medina	
Fernan Sanchez de Medina Constanza Alvarez de Moya	
Pedro Gomez Medina Juana Sanchez Aranda	
Luis Medina	Gil Fdz de Sotomayor Marina Fernandez Gadea
Luis Gomez de Medina	**Catalina de Sotomayor**
Maria Medina Aranda Rodrigo de Mendoza	
Geronimo Mendoza Catalina Mendoza	
Marina Mendoza Fernando de la Cerda	
Rodrigo de la Cerda	

Direct Medina line from the transcript.

I discovered a second manuscript, the investigation for Don Sancho Aranda in the year 1548. This manuscript *"Discurso Genealogico del Linaje de los Aranda Que Viven en la Cuidad de Alcala la Real"*, is consistent with the Joaquin Aranda investigation in 1748. There is a slight difference between the two. The latter investigation does not lift information from 1548. Manuscripts excerpts:

1. "Pedro Fernandez Aranda, first with this name, son of Domingo Romero."

2. "He married in the lifetime of his father with the daughter of Pascual Sanchez, Adalid del Rey. They lived in villa de Martos." *Adalid is a military position like captain. Pascual de Sanchez was a conquistador of Martos- he's memorialized.*

3. "They had three sons: Juan Sanchez de Aranda, Gonzalo Sanchez de Aranda and a daughter named Juana Sanchez de Aranda."

4. "Conquista de Alcala ano de 1341."

5. "Pedro Aranda died in 1413 at the age of 93."

6. "Juana Sanchez de Aranda, daughter of Don Pedro Fernandez de Aranda, the first, married Don Pedro Gomez de Medina, Alcayde de Priego, persona noble y principal."

7. "They had two sons, two names I can't remember and two daughters named Maria Diaz de Medina and the other Juana Gomez de Medina."

8. "Luis Gomez de Medina, grandson of Doña Juana Sanchez de Aranda and Alcayde Pedro Gomez de Medina, her husband. He married Doña Catalina de Sotomayor, sister of Alcayde Fernan de Alvarez. They procreated Don Diego de Medina and Doña Marina, who married in Baeza with Ruy Diaz de Mendoza. She was the mother of Geronimo de Mendoza, a page for the Duque de Sesa Don Luis de Cordova." *Mentions Geronimo's involvement in Italy.*

9. "Luis Gomez de Medina died and Doña Catalina, his wife, married a second time to Pedro Cardenes, Alcayde de Lucena."

Alvar de Medina	
Fernan Sanchez de Medina Constanza Alvarez de Moya	
Pedro Gomez Medina Juana Sanchez	
Luis Medina	Gil Fdz de Sotomayor Marina Fernandez Gadea
Luis Gomez de Medina	**Catalina de Sotomayor**
Maria Medina Aranda Rodrigo de Mendoza (b. 1450)	
Juan Mendoza (b.1490) Ana Negral (b. 1500)	
Ruy Diaz Mendoza (b. 1515) Catalina Salazar (b. 1527)	
Madalena Mendoza (b. 1545)	Vicente de Zaldivar

Madalena Mendoza to Alvar Medina

9 Sotomayor

Gil Fernandez de Sotomayor was Doña Maria de Medina's maternal grandfather. There are some empiezas to draw some genealogy. They are based pleito de hidalgos and noticias etc. The Sotomayors were descendants of Garcia Mendez de Sotomayor conquistador of Cordoba and the first Señor of Carpio.

I. Empieza en Gil Fernandez de Sotomayor

1. He was a in the Caballero de la Banda and Alcaide de Priego. This line ends with his 5th great grandson Pedro de Hoces y de Gongora, Señor de Albaida y Familiar de Santo Oficio.

2. Gil Fernandez de Sotomayor was married to Marina Fernandez de Gadea, daughter of the Domingo Garcia de Gadea. He was a natural of de Nava de Losa. He was one of the pobladores and conquistadors of Alcala la Real.

3. Their daughter Doña Catalina Gadea de Sotomayor married Pedro de Cardenas, Alcaide. *Her first husband is not identified.*

All this genealogical information is consistent with the Aranda manuscripts.

II. Empieza en Gomez de Sotomayor
1. He is a vecino de Alcaraz (Albacete). This line ends with his 8th great grandson Jose de Sotomayor y Zapata, XII Señor de Bucor, Alferez Mayor de Alcala de Real (Jaen). Jose de Sotomayor y Zapata is a direct descendant of Gil Fernandez de Sotomayor. This empieza shows Gomez de Sotomayor as the father of Gil Fernandez de Sotomayor.
2. Gomez de Sotomayor, vecino of Alcaraz, he is mentioned in the *Historia de Corona*. He was the son of Luis Mendez, Señor de Carpio, and Catalina Sanchez Manuel. He married Maria de Fernandez and their son was Gil Fernandez de Sotomayor.
3. Gil Fernandez Sotomayor arrived from Alcaraz to Cordoba to serve as Alcaide. He was a Caballero in the Order of Banda. He married Marina Fernandez Gadea, daughter of Hernan Luis de Gadea, Alcaide de Alcala.

A contradiction between the two empiezas exist as to who is the father of Marina de Gadea. Hernan is probably her father. Domingo de Gadea as poblador does not fit in the time frame. Domingo de Gadea was a conquistador of Alcala la Real.

On the Sotomayor paternal lineage chart on the next page, two of the women are descendants of the Temez family. Urraca Alfonso Cordoba was the daughter of Alfonso Fernandez de Cordoba and Teresa Ximenez Gongora.

Temez Family is discussed in the next chapter.

Sancha Juana Ruiz Jodar was the daughter of Sancho Perez, son of Sancho Martinez de Jodar. He is discussed in the following chapters. Sancha de Jodar is often named as a daughter of Adelantando Sancho Martinez de Jodar, but is likely a granddaughter.

Guiomar Haro Baeza was the daughter of Lope Ruiz Baeza, Señor de Guardia. She had a sister named Sancha Ponce who married the Señor de Oñate. They both are mentioned in their father's testament in the year 1340. According to some researchers they were descendants of Alfonso's IX daughter Aldonza de León and Pedro Ponce Cabrera. In my research there are some contradictions on how they descend from Alfonso IX. I could not come to a definite conclusion.

Garcia Mendez Sotomayor **Ynes Saavedra**	
Alonso Garcia Sotomayor *Urraca Alonso Fernandez*	
Garcia Mendez Sotomayor Sancha Juana Ruiz Jodar	
Luis Gomez Sotomayor Guiomar Baeza Haro	
Garcia Mendez Maria Fernandez Cordoba	
Luis Mendez Sotomayor Catalina Sanchez Manuel	
Gomez Sotomayor Maria Fernandez	
Gil Fdz Sotomayor Marina Fdz Gadea	
Catalina Sotomayor Luis Medina	
Maria Medina	**Rodrigo Mendoza**
	Juan Mendoza Ana Negral
Catalina Salazar	Ruy Diaz Mendoza

Sotomayor Lineage

10 VILLODRE

Catalina Manuel de Villodre was the daughter of Garcia Fernandez de Villodore and Doña Ines Manuel de Villena. Catalina Manuel married Luis Mendez de Sotomayor, Señor de Carpio.

Ines Manuel de Villena was the daughter of Fernan Sanchez Manuel and Elvira Sanchez. She married Garcia Fernandez Villodre and procreated two children: Elvira and Catalina.

Elvira married Mosen Enrique de Cribel, son of Guillaume Cribel and Amice de Serdobal. Enrique and Ines were the founders of the convento Sancti Spiritus for nuns and Santo Domingo de Alcaraz for friars. Enrique left a last testament in Alcaraz on June 6, 1424. His sepulchre reads:

"AQUI IACE EL HONRADO CAVALLERO MOSSEN/ENRIQVE CRIBEL FVNDADOR DESTE CONVENTO/DE LA CASA DEL REY DE FRANCIA"

Garcia Fernandez de Villodre was a prisoner in Monitel for his support of Pedro I during the civil war. He was granted a pardon by Enrique II and his goods were restituted to him and his wife. He was a descendant of Don Ruy Garcia de Villodre a conquistador of Seville. He served as Copero

Mayor and Mayordomo for Sancho Alfonso de Castilla, Conde de Alburquerque, son of Alfonso XI of Castile.

	Fernando III de Castile (1199-1252) & Elizabeth de Swabia (1205-1235)
	Infante Manuel (1234-1283)
	Sancho Manuel
	Fernan Manuel Sanchez & Elvira Sanchez
Garcia Fernandez de Villodre	Ines Manuel Villena
Catalina Villodre	

Catalina Villodre maternal lineage

Noticias:

9.06.1367. Carta del Rey Pedro I a Garci Fernandez de Villodre, en la que trata de various asunto relacionados con los impuestos que debe paga la ciudad de Cuenca.

02.02.1369. Toledo. Orden dada por los Alcaldes a Diego Martinez, contador de la Casa de la Moneda de dicha Ciudad, para entregue a Don Garcia Fernandez de Villodre, mayordomo mayor de don Sancho, conde de Alburquerque, cierta cantidad de la que tenia depositada don Vasco Fernandez de Toledo, arzobispo de dicha Ciudad, 0-6,f 127

v. N 65304 del inventario. Doc.

05.15.1369. Illescas. Carta de la reina doña Juana de Manuel, ordenando que se ampara a doña Ines Fernandez, mujer de Garcia Fernandez de Villodre, para que puede hacer viaje para encontrarse con ella. M-46, f 112. N 52102 del inventario. Doc.

03.28.1383. Tordesillas. Extracto de la provision del Rey Juan II, por la que ordena se paguen a doña Ines Fernandez, viuda de Garcia Fernandez de Villodre, ciertos maravedis en recompensa de la salinas de Pinilla. M-46, f 122 v. N 52104 del inventario. Doc.

10.03.1413. Real sobre Balaguer Carta del rey de Aragón, Fernando I, a los del consejo de su sobrino, el Rey Juan II de Castilla, en recomendacion de doña Elvira Sanchez de Villodre, mujer de mosen Enrique Cribel. M-46, f113. N 52105 del inventario. Doc.

10.18.1365. Sevilla. Carta del rey Pedro I a Garci Fernandez de Villodre, en la que trata de cierta merced que le ha hecho en las salinas de Monteagudo, reparos y envio de ingenios de artilleria al castillo de Moya, y otros asuntos. M-46, f 107. N 52096 del inventario. Doc.

05.22.1367. Madrid. Provision del Rey Pedro I por la que ordena que las rentas de los bienes que ha destinado a su hijo, Sancho de Castilla, sean entregadas a su mayordomo mayor, Garci Fernandez de Villodre. M-46, f 107 y 107 v. N 52097 del inventario. Doc.

08.00.1362. Real Sobre Calatayud Carta de privilegio del rey Pedro I por la que hace merced de cierta renta a Garcia

Fernandez de Villodre, copero mayor, de su hijo, don Alfonso, infante primero y heredero. M-46, f 107 v. y 108. N 52098 del inventario. Doc.

Si ano. 01.28. Real sobre Palenzuela Provision del rey Pedro I a los concejos de Alcaraz, Ubeda, Santisteban del Puerto y otros, para que ayuden a Garcia Fernandez de Villodre en lo que les pida, para cosas de su servicio. M-46, f 105. N 52092 del inventario. Doc.

04.09.1408. Alcala de Henares, Cedula del rey Juan II por la que ordena pagar a doña Elvira Sanchez de Villodre ciertas cantidades que se debian a su padre, don Garcia Sanchez de Villodre. M-46, f 36 a 38. N 52062 del inventario. Doc.

08.01.1379. Burgos Cedula del rey Juan I por la que ordena pagar a doña Ines de Manuel, mujer de Garcia Sanchez de Villodre. M-46. f 38 v. y 39. N 52063 de inventario. Doc.

Carpio
[136] 1356. Pedro I (1350-1369) ordena ciudades y villas de Andalucia que asisten a Don Garcia Fernandez de Villodre para tomar el castillo de Segura (Jaen).
C. 80-8

[137] 1356. Pedro I concede a Garcia Fernandez de Villodre los bienes que Gomez Carrillo y sus parciales dejaron en el Adelantamiento de Cazorla.
C. 80-3.

[138] 1356. Pedro I concede la tenencia de fortalezas a Garcia Fernandez de Villodre.
C. 2-3

[139] 1369. Enrique II (1369-1379] restituye sus bienes a Garcia Fernandez de Villodre.
C. 2-4
[140] 1379, 1383. Juan I (1379) restituye sus bienes a la mujer de Garcia Fernandez de Villodre.
C. 80-9 y 10

Fernan Sanchez de Manuel married Elvira Sanchez and their children were Ines and Elvira. Fernan Sanchez Manuel died sometime in 1354. Elvira purchased Pinilla near Alcaraz in 1355. It is these purchase documents that Elvira is stated as the wife of Fernan Sanchez, son of Sancho Manuel, the son of Infante Manuel. Sancho Manuel's wife is unknown.

Noticias:
6.30.1355. Alcaraz. Venta en publica subasta de la villa de Pinilla, confiscada a Rodrigo Alvarez de Varea, por carta de rey Pedro I, fechada en Guadalupe el 21 de julio 1355, a favor de doña Elvira Sanchez, mujer de Fernan Sanchez de Manuel. M-46, f46 a 47 v. N 52070 del inventario. Doc.

9.01.1356. Alcaraz. Carta de pago de los maravedis por los que doña Elvira Sanchez, mujer de Fernan Sanchez Manuel, compro la villa de Pinilla. M-46, f 47 a 48 v. N 52070. Doc.

Infante Don Manuel's illegitimate children were: Fernan Manuel, Blanca, Sancho and a legitimate son Juan Manuel (Prince of Villena). Juan Manuel's various descendants, who are named Sancho, are often confused with his bastard brother Sancho (the ancestor of Catalina Villodre).

King Fernando II de León (1137-1188) was the father of Infante Manuel. He married Urraca of Portugal daughter of King Henry I of Portugal and Maud of Savoy.

	Infante Manuel	Beatris de Savoy
Sancho Manuel (bastard)		Juan Manuel Prince of Villena
Fernan Sanchez Elvira Sanchez		Sancho (bastard) Ines Diaz
Ines Manuel		Sancho Manuel
Catalina Villodre		

11 Valenzuela

The following is the paternal and maternal family lines of Doña Sancha Montemayor y Valenzuela. She has several lines of sangre real (royal blood). Her connection to these royal lines is not a stretch but it is well known and documented. Charts inserted for an easier understanding.

Payas Arias		
Martin Sanchez Castro	Urraca Valenzuela	E
Juan Perez Valenzuela	Aldonza de Castro	D
Martin Valenzuela	Sancha Porras Martinez	C
Juan Perez Valenzuela	Berenguela Montemayor	B
Alfonso Montemayor	Aldonza Narvaez	A
Sancha Montemayor	Rodrigo Mendoza	

Aldonza de Narvaez married Alfonso Montemayor son of Juan Perez Valenzuela and Berenguela de Montemayor. He inherited his father mayorazgo in the year 1429. According to Gonzalo Argote de Molina, Aldonza Narvaez was the daughter of Obispo Don Rodrigo de Narvaez. However, in a testimony given by Andres de Montemayor he stated that Sancha de Montemayor gave instruction in her will that

Don Rodrigo de Narvaez (1383-1422) was her uncle. Rodrigo was the son of Juan Ruiz Narvaez and Catalina Villaseca, daughter of Sancho de Villaseca.

Juan Ruiz Narvaez was the son of Pedro Lopez Narvaez and Teresa de Biedma, daughter of Rodrigo Iniguez Biedma and Juana Diaz Fines. In a noticia on 5/15/1369, Don Rodrigo Iniguez de Biedma stated he was a cousin to Don Sancho de Villaseca. Rodrigo Biedma was also his father in law.

The Narvaez surname originates from the casa de solar San Juan de Pie de Puerto in lower Navarre. They were also Señores de Benacason en la huerta in Valencia. It was Pero Lopez de Narvaez who went to frontier of Jaen. He is buried in capilla mayor of San Miguel de Baeza. His father was Inigo Ruiz de Narvaez was Señor de Benacacon y Benareduan in Valencia. He was also Alcaide of Jerica.

Juana Diaz de Sanchez was the wife of Rodrigo Iniguez de Biedma. She was the daughter of Diego Diaz de Sanchez and Juana Ruiz de Lopez and the granddaughter of Dia Sanchez and Teresa Gomez de Roa. Her grandfather was a conquistador of Cordoba and Adelantado of the frontier. He was said to be the brother of Sancho Martinez de Joder, Adelantando of the frontier. Diego de Sanchez had been confused with being from the Funes solar in Navarro. However, research confirms he used the surname Fines from a tower he conquered. He was the son of Sancho Fernandez and Teresa Diaz Haro, daughter of Diego Lopez de Haro II and Toda Perez. Sancho was the son of Fernando II and Urraca Lopez de Haro (confirmed by a document in 1214).

Noticias:

"Yo Diag sola merced de dios y de Santa Maria de Toledo gane Fines el castillo cerca de Valdeporchena, a servicio de de Dios e del cristianismo con con ayuda de mis amigos, dolo a la Igelsia de Toledo, e al Azobispo" ano 1242.

10/8/96. Valladolid. Fernando IV ordena devolver a Juana Diaz, hija de Diag Sanchez de Funes y mujer de Rodrigo Iniguez de Biedma, el cortijo de los Ardales, que le habia arrebatado Doña Fernan Perez Ponce, Adelantado de la Frontera por Sancho IV, para darselo a Fernan Gutierrez Quixada.

		Fernando II King of Leon
		Sancho Lord of Fines
		Dia Sanchez Conquistador de Cordoba (d.before 1260)
Sancho Narvaez		Diaz S Finez
Iniguez Narvaez	***Rodrigo Inguez Biedma***	Juana Fines 1296
Pero Lopez Narvaez	***Teresa Biedma***	
Juan Narvaez	Catalina Villaseca	
Paternal line	Maternal line	
Aldonza		

Maternal Line B: Berenguela Montemayor

Berenguela de Montemayor was the daughter of Martin Alfonso de Montemayor and probably Doña Maria de Carrillo y Cordoba. Martin Alfonso de Montemayor was IV Señor of Montemayor and testified in the year 1390. He did not mention Berenguela in his will. In 1397, Berenguela is named as the daughter Martin Alfonso de Montemayor in a dowry contract with Don Juan Perez de Valenzuela.

Martin Alfonso Montemayor was the son of Don Alonso Fernandez de Montemayor, III Señor de Montemayor y Dos Hermanas, and Doña Juana de Martinez. His siblings were: Fernando de Alfonso, Diego de Alfonso, Beatris de Alfonso, Constanza, Aldonza Lopez, Leonor Alfonso, and Maria Alfonso. His wife, Maria Carrillo Cordoba, was a cousin.

Alfonso de Montemayor, III Señor de Montemayor, was the son of Martin Alfonso, II Señor de Montemayor y los Dos Hermanas, and Aldonza Lopez. Aldonza was the daughter of Lope Gutierrez de Haro, Alcalde de Seville, and Doña Maria Garcia de Carrillo; granddaughter of Pedro Diaz Haro, Señor de Carcar, and Doña Leonor Fernandez de Castro; great-granddaughter of Diego Lopez de Haro and Toda Perez. Alfonso de Montemayor III testified in 6/29/1317 and died 7/8/1340. He was buried in Capilla de San Bartolome.

Martin Alfonso; II Señor de Montemayor, Alcaudete, Dos Hermanas; was the son of Alfonso Fernandez de Cordoba and Doña Teresa Jimenez de Gongora. He and his father were both Adelantado of the frontier of Andaluzia.

Alfonso de Cordoba (d. 1327) was the Señor de Canete, Los Dos Hermanas, and Cordoba. He was the son of Fernan Nunez Temez, conquistador of Cordoba, and doña Leonor Munoz. She was the daughter of the famous conquistador and Adalid Don Domingo de Munoz. He was a descendant of conquistadors and pobladores of Avila.

Fernan Nunez Temes (d. 1283) was a conquistador of Cordoba. He was granted by Fernando III the Senores of "los Castillos de Canete, Paterna, Loeches, Dos Hermanas, y el Lugar De Fernan Nunez, a que dio su nombre, y pobló de Christianos, y fue primer Señor de el." He renamed the defensive tower of Aben Hana which was seized June 29, 1236. His father Nuno Fernandez de Temes was the 4th Grand Master of the Order of Alcantara between the years of 1208-1219.

Nuno Fernandez, Grand Master of the Order of Alcantara, was the son of Vasco Fernandez. Vasco was the Señor del Castillo y solar de Temez y Chantada. He married Mayor de Nunez. He was the son of Fernan Bermudez de Trava and Urraca Fernandez de Temez, Señora de Temez y Chantada. Vasco was buried in the Abadia de Santiago de Losada del Obispado de Lugo, near Chantada. His sepulchre reads:
"Aqui jaz Basco Peres de Temes
Rico e Poderoso Cavaleiro.
Pequeo de corpo, mais avia muito seso,
Lealdade, e esforzo."
Fernan Bermudez de Trava was the son of Bermudez Trava ad Urraca Enriquez, daughter of Teresa de León, Queen of Portugal. Teresa was the illegitimate daughter of Alfonso VI and Jimena Munoz. The Temez family were known to be descendants of Alfonso VI, King of Leon. Ruy Diaz de

Mendoza descends from Urrace Enriquez and Henry I, King of Portugal, children of Teresa de León and Henry Count of Portugal.

	Alfonso VI (King of León)
	Teresa de León (Queen of Portugal) & Henry of Burgundy
Fernan Bermudez Trava	Urraca Enriquez
Vasco Fernandez Temez	Mayor Nunez
Nuno Fernandez Temez	Elvira de Castro
Fernan Nunez Temez	Leonor Munoz
Alfonso Fdz. Cordoba	Teresa Jimenez Gongora
Martin Alf. Montemayor	Aldonza Lopez
Alfonso Fdz. Montemayor	Juana Martinez
Martin Alf. Montemayor d. 1390	Maria Carrillo Cordoba
Berenguela Montemayor Married 1397	

Paternal ancestor (and wives) of Berenguela Montemayor

Inigo Lopez D. abt. 1076	Toda Ortiz
Lopez Iniguez d. 1093	Telca Diaz
Diego Lopez I de Haro d. abt. 1140	Maria Sanchez
Lope Diaz de Haro I d. 5/6/1170	Aldonza
Diego Lopez de Haro	Toda Perez
Pedro Diaz de Haro	
Lope Gutierrez de Haro	Juan Garcia Carrillo
Aldonza Lopez	

Paternal ancestry of Aldonza Lopez

Maternal Line D: Sancha Martinez de Porras

Sancha Martinez Porras was the daughter of Fernan de Porras and Doña Mayor Martinez de Argote. She married Martin Sanchez de Valenzuela and they had seven children. In early 1380, both requested to form a Mayorazgo. On April 27, 1380 the application was expedited by Juan I. Then again, on May 21, 1380 they requested to be buried in the church of San Pedro in the sepulchre of Alfonso Tello de Castro, great-grandfather of Don Martin Sanchez de Valenzuela. Their son Juan Perez de Valenzuela testified in 1429, that his father Martin Sanchez was married twice. Their son was Don Alonso Fernandez Valenzuela, father of Doña Sancha de Montemayor, he died in Linares in March 12, 1441.

	Fernan Porras Maria Martinez Argote
Martin Sanchez Valenzuela	Sancha Martinez Porras

Maternal Lineage E: Aldonza de Castro

Aldonza de Castro was the daughter of Tello Alfonso de Castro. She married her relative Juan Perez de Valenzuela. The testimony of Martin Sanchez states Tello Alfonso de Castro was his great-grandfather. Tello Alfonso de Castro was a conquistador of Cordoba.

	Tello Alfonso de Castro
Juan Perez Valenzuela	Aldonza de Castro

Maternal Lineage F: Urraca Valenzuela

Urraca Valenzuela was the daughter of Don Juan Perez de Valenzuela, Señor de Valenzuela. Juan Perez was the son of Pedro Sanchez de Valenzuela, Alcalde Mayor de Baena. She married Martin Sanchez de Castro, son of Pay Arias de Castro and Urraca Tellez de Meneses. Urraca and Martin were the parents of: Juan Perez de Valenzuela, successor; Ruy Gonzalez de Castro, Caballero de Banda; Gonzalo Martinez de Castro, Caballero del Orden de Calatrava.

Pay Arias Castro, father of Martin Sanchez de Castro, was conquistador of Cordoba and Señor de Espejo. His wife was Doña Urraca Alfonso Tellez de Meneses. The ancestry of Pay Arias de Castro is unsettled. There are theories but nothing conclusive. He was from Castroviejo, Spain. His mother was Maria de Lopez and siblings were Mencia and Lope Lopez. His other child was Ruy Paez. On May 17, 1315 in Cordoba, Pay gave lease to his son Ruy for Espejo. He married doña Teresa Martinez and she gave her last testament in Cordoba on September 12, 1361. Pay Arias de Castro is the direct paternal ancestor of Doña Sancha de Montemayor.

Juan Perez de Valenzuela, father doña Urraca, was Señor of Valenzuela y Castillo. He was Alcalde y Alcalde Mayor de Baena. His wife is unknown.

Pedro Sanchez Valenzuela, father of Juan Perez, was Señor of Valenzuela. He was Alcalde Mayor of Baena, and Luque. He married Urraca and were the parents of Sancho Perez and the mentioned Juan Perez de Valenzuela. He was said to be the nephew of Sancho Martinez, Señor de Jodar.

Lope Sanchez, father of Pedro Sanchez Valenzuela, was the first Señor of Valenzuela, conquistador of Cordoba and Camarero de Mayor of Fernando III. Supposedly, Lope Sanchez was married to Doña Sancha Alfonso de León, daughter of Rodrigo Alfonso de León and Ines Rodriguez de Cabrera. I have not found anything to substantiate this claim. More research is needed on Sancha Alfonso.

Sancho Fernandez de León (1186-8/25/1220). He was the father of Lope Sanchez. He was the son of Ferdinand II of León and Doña Urraca Lopez de Haro (b. 1160-d. 1230). Sancho's maternal grandparents were Lopez Diaz I, Señor de Vizcaya and Aldonza Rodriguez. He married Doña Teresa Diaz de Haro, daughter of Diego Lopez Haro II and Toda de Perez. They were the parents of: Maria, Diego

Sanchez de Fines, and Lope Sanchez de Leon.

Fernando II King of Leon	Urraca Lopez de Haro
Sancho Fernandez de Leon	Teresa Diaz de Haro
Lope Sanchez de Leon	*Sancha Alfonso de Leon*
Pedro Sanchez	Urraca
Juan Perez de Valenzuela	unknown
Urraca Valenzuela	Martin Sanchez de Castro

Paternal ancestors of Urraca Valenzuela

Final conclusion: The mystery of Ruy Diaz de Mendoza is finally solved through genealogical method and document research. This case was "everything is in details" type case. I can say with certainty he was the son of Juan Mendoza, Caballero of the Order of Santiago, and that Doña Ana Hernandez Negral was probably his mother. His descent from Queen Urraca de León, Fernando II, and Ferdinand III, as provided in the previous pages, is the strongest evidence of his sangre real. There are other claims of sangre real in other lateral lineages, but I can't say with certainty that those claims are valid. His relationship with Marques de Mondejar is distant kinship and nothing more.

-Levi Villarreal

July 20, 2016

Fernando II de Leon	Urraca Lopez de Haro
Sancho Fernandez	Teresa Diaz de Haro
Lope Sanchez	Sancha Alfonso de Leon
Pedro Sanchez	Urraca
Juan Perez Valenzuela	
Urraca Valenzuela	Martin Sanchez de Castro
Juan Perez Valenzuela	Aldonza Castro
Martin Valenzuela	Sancha Porras Martinez
Juan Perez Valenzuela	Berenguela Montemayor
Alfonso Montemayor	Aldonza Narvaez
Sancha Montemayor	Rodrigo Mendoza
Rodrigo	Maria Medina
Juan Mendoza	Ana Hernandez Negral
Ruy Diaz de Mendoza	Catalina Salazar

Ruy Diaz Mendoza line to Fernando II

Fernando II de Leon

Alfonso IX	Sancho
Fernando III Aldonza Martinez	Diego de Fines and brother Lope Sanchez de Leon
Rodrigo Alfonso	
Sancha Alfonso	

Fernando III de Castile

Manuel
Sancho (Bastard) not to be confused with Sancho Lord of Carrion
Fernan Sanchez Elvira Sanchez
Ines Manuel Garcia Villodre
Catalina Villodre

Diego Lopez de Haro

Lope Ruiz de Haro Senor de Guardia	Teresa Diaz Haro Queen of Leon	Pedro Diaz Haro

Three ancestors of Ruy Diaz de Mendoza

Queen of Portugal Teresa de León

1. Urraca Enriquez Bermudo Traba	2. Henry King of Portugal
Fernando Bermudez Traba Urraca Fernandez Temez	Urraca Fernando II Leon
Vasco Fernandez de Temes	
Nuno Fernandez (Señor de Temez y Chantada) 4th Grand Master of the Alcantara (1208-1219) & Elvira Fernandez de Castro	
Fernan Nunez de Temez (Conquistador de Cordoba) & Leonor Munoz or Ora Munoz Progenitors of the Fernandez de Cordoba Family	

Mendoza Family Tree

Rodrigo de Mendoza, conquistador of Baeza, Spain. He married Leonor Alonso de Godoy, daughter of Pero de Godoy. Children:

Juan de Mendoza. He married Juana Garcia de Cardenas, daughter of Sancho Garcia de Cardenas. Children:

Juan Lopez de Mendoza, Justicia Mayor de Baeza. Children:

Juan de Mendoza married Doña Isabel Rodriguez Peralta. Children:

Rodrigo de Mendoza, El Bueno, married Doña Sancha Montemayor. Their children were Leonor de Mendoza and Rodrigo.

Rodrigo de Mendoza, married Doña Maria de Medina. He went to Granada with the Marques de Mondejar. He had three children.
  A. Juan de Mendoza
  B. Diego de Mendoza
  C. Geronimo de Mendoza

A. Juan de Mendoza, el Caballero de Orden de Santiago. He married Doña Ana Hernandez de Negral. She was a noble-woman, she was likely a descendant of the conquistadors of Granada.
Children: Ruy Diaz de Mendoza and Simon Mendoza.

A1. Ruy Diaz de Mendoza, birthdate unknown. He died after 1545, in New Spain. He married Catalina de Salazar, before 1540, she was the daughter of Factor Gonzalo de Salazar and Catalina de Cadena.
Children: Ana, Madalena, Ruy Diaz de Mendoza.

A1.1 Madalena Mendoza (abt. 1543) was born in Granada. She married Teniente de Capitán General Vicente de Zaldivar. He was born in Vitoria, Spain.
Children: Vicente, Juan, and Madalena.

A1.1.2. Madalena Mendoza was born in Zacatecas, Mexico. She married Juan Guerra Reza. He was Teniente de Capitán General of New Mexico. They both financed the conquest of her uncle's, Adelantado Juan de Oñate, conquest of New Mexico. Juan de Oñate was the half brother of Madalena's mother.
Children: Vicente de Zaldivar.

A1.1.2.1 Vicente de Zaldivar. He was born in Zacatecas, Mexico. He married Ana de Sosa. She was the daughter of Alferez Alonso de Farias and Maria Sosa. Maria de Soas was a descendant of conquistador Andres de Tapia, a conqueror of the Aztec Empire.
Children: Agustin, Vicente, Margarita, Maria, Mariana, and Ana.

A1.1.2.1.1 Margarita de Sosa y Zaldivar married Diego de Ayala, Teniente de Capitan General de Nuevo Leon, he was the son of conquistador Joseph de Trevino and Leonor de Ayala. They married in Monterrey, Nuevo Leon in 1653.
Children: Margarita and Ines.

Dispensation excerpt:

"The witness knows that Captain Don Vicente de Zaldivar y Reza, legitimate son Juan Guerra de Reza and Doña Madalena de Mendoza, legitimate daughter of General Vicente Zaldivar and Doña Madalena Mendoza, vecinos de Zacatecas" -Pablo Sanchez

A1.1.2.1.2 Mariana de Sosa married Don Diego Garcia de Quintanilla, son of conquistador Lucas Garcia and Juliana Quintanilla, in Monterrey, Nuevo Leon.
Children: Agustina, Gaspar, Josefa, Vicente, Maria, Thomas, Gertrudis, Diego.

Excerpt from the marriage dispensation of Agustina Garcia and Pedro Longoria:
Monterrey, Nuevo Leon. January 23, 1678.
"It's public knowledge she is a descendant of the first conquistadors of the kingdom (Nuevo León). And she is the granddaughter of Don Vicente Zaldivar y Resa on her mother's side." -Pedro Longoria

A2. Ruy Diaz de Mendoza was born in Granada, Spain. He married Maria Velasco, daughter of Don Francisco Perez Velasco. Ruy was Veinte Cuatro of Granada, Procurador of the Cortes, and Tesorero de Casa Moneda in Mexico City. He died sometime after 1579. No known children.

B. Diego Mendoza married Ynes Farfana. Diego was born in Baeza. He was a camarero for the Marques de Mondejar. He died before 1546. He married Ynes Farfana. She was the daughter of Doña Leonor Farfana. Her father is unknown. She was literate and a noble woman from Seville, Spain. She owned a store in Belicena. She later sold it to her daughter Leonor and moved to Baeza.

Children: Diego, Leonor, Juan and Geronimo.

B1. Diego Mendoza sailed to New Spain after November 29, 1553. He was a criado of the Archbishop of Mexico Alonso de Montufar Y Bravo de Lagunas. Excerpts from limpieza de sangre sometime October, 1553:

"Diego Mendoza a vecino de abad Granada. The witness knows Diego de Mendoza, father of Diego de Mendoza, and Ynes de Farfana, his wife. They were married according to the church. The said parents procreated their legitimate son Diego de Mendoza. They were hijosdalgos notorios."
-Don Francisco ...escudero

It is unknown what became of Diego de Mendoza after his arrival in New Spain.

B2. Leonor Mendoza married Sebastian de Coca Trivino. They both purchased the business of Ynes de Farfana. The business involved the storage and selling of wine. Children: Maria de Mendoza and Ines de Mendoza.

B2.1. Ines Mendoza married Fernando de Bedoya and they procreated a daughter named Francisca de Mendoza. She sailed to Peru in 1606.

B2.2. Maria Mendoza Coca married Fernando de Torres y Portugal. They sailed to Peru in 1606. Children: Diego de Diego and Luis de Torres.

B2.2.1. Luis de Torres y Portugal was a natural of Paz, Peru. He married Doña Marcela de Montellano, a natural of Lima. She was the daughter of Andres de Montellano and Doña Petronila de Pineda.

Children: Agustin, Luisa, Fernando and Andres.

B2.2.1.1 Agustin de Torres y Portugal, caballero de Orden de Santiago. Excerpts of the limpieza de sangre:
Antonio de Leiva:
1. "His paternal grandparents were named Fernando de Torres y Portugal and Maria de Coca Trivino y Mendoza, naturals of Jaen.
2. They are caballeros hijodalgos notorios de sangre and the candidate descends from the male line of the Conde de Villardompardo, Viceroy of Peru.

Madrid, same day, month and year. Marcelo de Ayala:
1. The candidate is the great grandson of the Conde de Villardompardo, Viceroy and Captain General of Peru. Don Fernando received the encomienda de Guarina.

The records produced for the Limpieza:

March 3, 1616. Cathedral de Nuestra Señora de Paz. Bapt. Luis, 13 days, son of Maestre de Campo Don Fernando de Torres y Portugal and Maria Coca Trivino de Mendoza. Padrinos: General Agustin Sarmiento de Sotomayor y Doña Leonor de Merino.

Testament of Fernando de Torres y Portugal:
"In the name of God Amen. I Don Fernando de Torres y Portugal, natural of the city of Jaen in Spain, encomendero in Peru; and son of Diego de Torres y Portugal, caballero de orden de Santiago, and Doña Isabel Maria Carrillo y Mendoza, my deceased parents. I contracted marriage with Doña Maria de Coca Trivino y Mendoza, daughter of Don Sebastian Coca y Trivino and Doña Leonor de Mendoza."

Diego De Torres Y Portugal was Captain of the Infantry and died during the war in Flanders. He was natural son.

Parish of Santa Maria, Jaen
"December 9, 1561. Bapt. Maria, daughter of Sebastian de Coca Trivino and Doña Leonor de Mendoza, his wife. Compadres: Andres de Baeza and Doña Teresa de Gamez."

June 22, 1568. Bapt. Fernando, a natural son of Diego de Torres y Portugal and a single woman.
Compadres: Lic. Huerta and Doña Cathalina de Balmaseda.

Testament:
"Yo Diego de Torres Y Portugal, Caballero del Orden de Santiago, the legitimate son of el Don Fernando de Torres y Portugal and Doña Francisca Carvajal."

This male line was a direct descendant of the kings of Portugal. The evidence can be found in Don Fernando de Torres y Portugal's grandfathers limpieza de sangre for the order of Santiago. They descend from Infante Denis, son of King Peter I of Portugal and Ines de Castro.

B3. Juan Mendoza was born in Granada. He married Doña Maria Carvajal, daughter of Don Alonso de Carvajal, from Baeza. Secondly, he married Doña Mayor de Castro. Children with Maria Carvajal: Ines and Isabel Ana.

B3.1. Ines de Carvajal, monja de Abito de Santiago in Granada (for nobles).

B3.2. Isabel Ana de Mendoza married Luis Carrillo, son of Cristobal Carrillo Carvajal and Catalina Aranda.

Children: Luis Carrillo Carvajal, Abito de Santiago. 1588.

C. Geronimo de Mendoza was born in Baeza. He served as page for the Duke of Sesa (Luis Cordoba). He participated in the war of Pavia. He spent time in corregimiento of Avila and was Regidor of Baeza. He married Doña Catalina de Mendoza, daughter of Rodrigo Mendoza de Carvajal and Sancha Mendoza.
Children: Marina Mendoza

C1. Marina Mendoza married Fernando Mesia de la Cerda, V Señor de la Vega y Armijo. He was the son of Luis Mesia de la Cerda, IV Señor de la Vega y Armijo.
Children: Beatris and Rodrigo.

C1.1. Beatris de la Cerda married Don Martin de Ceron Benavides. He served in spanish galleys, Abito de Santiago, Veinticuatro de Jaen,
Children: Juan Ceron de la Cerda, Abito de Santiago

C1.2. Rodrigo de la Cerda, Abito de Calatrava y Santiago, veinticuatro, VI Senor de la Vega y Armijo. His descendant Don Pedro Messia de la Cerda was the the Viceroy of New Granada (1761-1773).

BIBLIO
Rivadeneira de Oñate, Francisco; Pruebas para la concesion del
Titulo de Caballero de la Orden de Santiago; Consejo de Ordenes
Archive Historico Nacional
ES.28079.AHN/1.1.13.8.4//OM-Caballeros_Santiago,

Zaldivar, Vicente de; Pruebas para la concesion del Titulo de la
Caballero de la Orden de Santiago; Consejo de Ordenes,
Archivo Historico Nacional ES.2809.AHN/1.1.13.8.4//OM
Caballeros Santiago, Exp.9070

Ceron de la Cerda, Juan; Pruebas para la concesion del Titulo de
Caballero de la Orden de Santiago de Juan Ceron de la Cerda, 1615,
Consejo de Ordenes, Archivo Historico Nacional, Es.
28079.AHN/1.1.13.8.4//OM-CABALLEROS_SANTIAGO,
EXP.1901

Carvajal y Mendoza, Luis; Pruebas para la concesion del Titulo de
Caballero de la Orden de Santiago, 1588, Consejo de Ordenes,
Archivo Historico Nacional, ES.28709.AHN/1.1.13.8.4.//OM-
CABALLEROS_SANTIAGO, Exp.1653

Biedma y Carvajal y Valenzuela, Sancho; Pruebas para la concesion
del Titulo de Caballero de la Orden de Santiago, 1559, Consejo de
Ordenes, Archivo Historico Nacional, ES.28079.AHN/1.1.13.8.4//
OM-CABALLEROS_SANTIAGO, Exp.1090.

Coleccion de don Luis de Salazar y Castro, Madrid: Real Academia
de la Historia.

Recopilacion Segunda de los Papeles Para la Genealogia por los
Apellidos: Toledo, Palomeque, Funes y Biedma. [Manuscrito]
Real Academia de la Historia-Signatura: 9/312, f91 a final-Signatura
antigua: D-37, f 91 a final

Noticias y Documentos Para la Historia de Baeza, Fernando Cozar
Martinez, ©1883.

Copias de varios testamentos y otros documentos, solicitadas a
instancia de Antonio [Dominguez Fernandez] de Cordoba [Lasso I]
marques de Valenzuela, Seccion Nobleza del Archivo Historico
Nacional, ES.45168.SNAHN/5.2.12/Luque, C. 767, D.38. Includes:
Copia del testamento otorgado por Martín Sánchez de Valenzuela y Sancha
Martínez de Porras, por el que fundaron mayorazgo en Valenzuela (Córdoba) en
cabeza de Juan Pérez Valenzuela, su hijo. Fecha del documento a 21 de mayo de
1418.-Copia del testamento de Juan Pérez de Valenzuela, hijo mayor de Martín
Sánchez de Valenzuela, dejando como heredero a su hijo Alfonso Fernández de
Valenzuela y sus nietos. Fecha del testamento 12 de marzo de 1429.-Copia de la
carta de dote otorgada por Juan Pérez de Valenzuela a favor de su mujer,
Berenguela Alfon en 18 de mayo de 1397.-Copia de la Real Cédula de Juan I a
favor de Martín Sánchez de Valenzuela para fundar mayorazgo en la villa de
Valenzuela (Córdoba). Fecha de 27 de abril de 1380.-Copia del testamento de
Alonso Sánchez de Valenzuela, veinticuatro de Córdoba, segundo hijo de Martín
Sánchez de Valenzuela y Sancha Martín de Porras, su mujer, dejando como
heredero a su hermano Juan Pérez de Valenzuela. Fecha de 12 de junio de
1420.-Copia del testamento de Alfonso Fernández de Valenzuela, veinticuatro de
Córdoba, nieto de Martín Sánchez de Valenzuela, hijo de Alfonso Sánchez de
Valenzuela, por el que deja como herederos a sus hijos. Fecha de 22 de
noviembre de 1445.

Memorial de Martin Ceron de Benavides, procurador por
Jaen. Archivo General de Simancas (Valladolid, Espana)
ES.47161.AGS/4.2.86//PTR,LEG,8, DOC.295

Señor Don Rodrigo de la Cerda Mendoza, Cordoba April 28, 1608,
Archivo Municipal de Cordoba, Pruebas de nobleza de Caballeros
Veinticuatros 1598-1642, cajas 23-24.

Torres y Portugal y de Montellano, Agustin, Consejo de Ordenes,
Archivo Historico Nacional, ES.28079.AHN/1.1.13.8.4//OM
Caballeros Santiago, Exp.8711, 1710.

Fernando Alvarez de Sotomayor, Real Provision Ejecutoria de
Hidalguia, Archivo de la Real Chancilleria, Signatura 4500-001, Caja
04500, Pieza 001, Antequera, 1530-02-28.

Pleito Entre de Fernando de Mendoza y de la Cerda, de Cordoba, Con Jeronimo de Mendoza, Fundar el Mayorazgo Que Ofrecen Los Segundos en la Capitulacion de Una Hija, Catalogo de Pleitos de la Real Audiencia y Chancilleria de Granada, Signatura, Caja 2350, Pieza 008, 1561.

Un Sanjuanista del Siglo XIV: Don Diego Sanchez de Finez Gran Prior de Castilla de León, Carlos Zavala Oyague, © 2014.

La Descendencia del Infante Don Manuel Y El Señorio de Pinilla, Juan de Torres Fontes, University of La Rioja, © 2003.

Un Gran Señor Medieval: Don Juan Manuel, Gregorio Sanchez Doncel, © 1982.

Historia genealogica y heraldica de la Monarquia, española, casa real y grandes de espana, Don Francisco de Bethencourt, Madrid © 1905.

Discurso Genealogico del Linaje de los Aranda que viven en la Cuidad de Alcala la Real, Lic. Sancho de Aranda, en ano 1548. [Manuscrito] Copiose en Granada de su original de mandado de Juan Altamirano y Carvajal por Joseph Bentura de Roxas Cortazero.

Nobleza de Andalucia: Que Dedico al Rey Don Felipe II, Gonzalo Argote de Molina, 1588. Copia digital: realizado por Biblioteca de Andalucia, Manuel Munoz y Garnica 1866 ed. Lit.

Escritura de Venta de un Cortijo Llamado de Torrubia, en Termino de Baeza(Jaen), Otorgada por Rui Diaz de Mendoza a Favor de Dia Sanchez de Quesada e Ines Padilla. Seccion Nobleza del Archivo Nacional 1495-11-16; ES.45168.SNAHN/6.59.3.1//BAENA, C.315, D.12

El Libro de Diezmos de Donadios de la Catedral de Cordoba, Universidad de Granada, Manuel Nieto Cumplido, © 1979

Vicisitudes de un Señorío de Frontera. Espejo (1304-1382), Universidad de Cordoba, Emilio Cabrera Munoz, ©2009

Empieza en Gomez de Sotomayor, Tabla Genealogica de la Familia Sotomayor, Vecina de Alcala la Real(Jaen). [Manuscrito] Real Academia de la Historia-Signatura: 9/306, folio 161- Signatura antigua: D-31, Folio 161

Empieza en Luis Mendez de Sotomayor y Fernandez de Villodore Hijo de los VI Senores de el Carpio. Tabla Genealogica de la Familia de Sotomayor, Marqueses de Melin, Vecina de Alcazar.[Manuscrito] Real de Academia de la Historia-Signatura 9/306. Folio 157v.- Signatura antigua: D-31, Folio 157v.

Empieza Martin Alfonso de Cordoba V Senor de Dos Hermanas y Segundo Nieto del Cabeza de la Tabla N26405, Tabla Genealogica de la Familia de Cordoba, Señores de Montemayor. [Manuscrito]Real de Academia de la Historia-Signatura 9/306, f67-Signatura antigua: D-31, f67.

Noticias de Algunos Señores de la Familia de Villodre. [Manuscrito] Real Academia de la Historia-Signatura: 9/306, folio 168.-Signatura Antigua: D-31, Folio 168.

Linages de Baeza, Un Volumen en 4 grado, Encuadernado en Pergamino, con 218 Hojas. [Manuscrito} Antonio Barahona Published 1499. Real Academia de la Historia-signatura: 9/194-Signatura Antigua: B-85

Linages de Baeza, Un Volumen en 4 grado, Encuadernado en Pergamino, con 218 Hojas. [Manuscrito} Carta de Don Antonio de Barahona, Published 1499. Real Academia de la Historia-Signatura: 9/194-Signatura Antigua: B-84.

Traslados del Testamento de Lope Ruiz de Baeza en el que Funda el Mayorazgo del La Guardia (Jaen) a Favor de su Hijo Juan Ruiz. Seccion Nobleza del Archivo Historico Nacional, Archivo de los Duques de Baena, BAENA, C.215, D.15-17

Memorial del Marques de la Vega, Luis Rodrigo Messia de la Cerda,

Al Rey Carlos II, Solicitando ser Mayordomo de Su Casa o Embajador en Turin. [Manuscrito] Real Academia-Signatura: 9/319, folio 147 a 148. El folio 148v. Esta Blanco-Signatura Antigua: D-45, folio 147 a 148v. Esta en blanco.

Tabla Genealogica de la Familia de Cordoba, Señores de Montemayor. [Manuscritos] Empieza en Martin Alfonso de Cordoba, V Señor de Dos Hermanas, Segundo Nieto del Cabeza de la Cabeza de la Tabla N 26405. Real Academia de la Historia-Signatura: 9/306, folio 67.- Signatura Antigua: D-31, Folio 67.

Ejecutoria del Pleito Litigado por Gutierre Negral, Vecino de Bernuy de Zapardiel (Avila), Con el Concejo, Justicia y Regimiento de Bernuy de Zapardiel (Avila) Sobre su Hidalguia, Archivo de la Real Chancilleria de Valladolid, ES.47186.ARCHV/8.7.1//Registro de Ejecutorias, Caja 816,12, 1554-10-27.

Ejecutoria del Pleito por Francisco Negral, Vecino de Segovia, con el Fiscal del Rey y el Concejo y Pecheros de Cuellar (Segovia), sobre, Archivo de la Real Chancilleria de Valladolid, ES.47186.ARCHV/ 8.7.1.//Registro de Ejecutorias, Caja 1217, 28, 1571-10-16.

Heraldica Y Genealogia en el Sureste de Cordoba (Ss. XIII-XIX), Oscar Barea Lopez. ISBN: 978-84-686-66079-0 Impreso en Espana, Editado por Bubok Publishing S.L. © 2014.

Lines of Descent from Alfonso XI, Rey de Castilla y Leon, to Ruy Diaz de Mendoza y Arellano, Jose Antonio de Esquibel. SHHAR (Vol. I, 1994).

La Descendencia del Infante Don Manuel y El Senorio de Pinilla, Juan Torres Fontes, © 2003.

Catalogo de Documentos Sobre Andalucia en El Archivo de la Casa Ducal de Alba (1335-1521), Esther Cruces Blanco, Del Cuerpo Facultativo de Archiveros y Bibliotecarios.

Linajes de Cordoba en Las Capillas Funerarias Medievales de la

Mezquita-Catedral, Maria Angeles Jordano Barbudo, Universidad de Cordoba, 2009.

La Mentira Como Arma. Pleitos en Torno a la Propiedad de un Mayorazgo. Ninchez Y Chozas (SS. XV-XVI), Maria Antonia Carmona Ruiz, Universidad de Sevilla, 2009.

Los protocolos notariales mas antiguos de Sante Fe: 1514-1549. Analisis y catalogo, Maria Amparo, Moreno Trujillo, © 1987. http://hdl.handle.net/10481/6374

Marriage Dispensation; Pedro de Longoria and Agustina Garcia "Mexico, Jalisco, registros parroquiales, 1590-1979," Insert datebases with images, family search (https://familysearch.org/pal:/MM9.3.1/TH-1-18409-35718-33?cc= 1874591), Guadalajara>Diocesis de Guadalajara> Matrimonios 1696-1697,1733>image163-168; parroquias, Catolicas, Jalisco(Catholic Church parishes, Jalisco).

Marriage Dispensation; Diego Ayala and Margarita Sosa "Mexico, Jalisco, registros parroquiales, 1590-1979,"Insert datebases with images, family search (http://familysearch.org/pal:/MM9.3.1/TH-1-18379-10963-7?cc=18 7459) Guadalajara>Diocesis de Guadalajara> Matrimonios 1638-1699>image 48 of 224; parroquias Catolicas, Jalisco (Catholic Church parishes, Jalisco).

Ruy Diaz de Mendoza

Levi